The Missing Piece:

Your School Resource Officer as an Ally in Parenting

The Missing Piece:

Your School Resource Officer as an Ally in Parenting

By

Dr. Beth J. Sanborn

The Missing Piece: Your School Resource Officer as an Ally in Parenting © 2022 by Dr. Beth J. Sanborn

To Andy, Greg, and Katie,
who have accepted that I have 4,800 other kids.

To my 4,800 Wiss kids,
this is for you!

Table of Contents

Introduction 9

Part I: Law Enforcement 21

    Chapter 1: SRO 101 23

    Chapter 2: Policing Through a Different Lens 35

    Chapter 3: Humanizing Policing 47

    Chapter 4: Bridging the Gap 55

    Chapter 5: Not Your Traditional Precinct 63

Part II: Informal Counselor/Mentor 71

    Chapter 6: Building Trust 73

    Chapter 7: Long-Term Relationship Building 79

    Chapter 8: Vulnerability 85

    Chapter 9: Advocating for Students 91

    Chapter 10: Leading by Example 97

    Chapter 11: Smiling is Contagious 101

Part III: Public Safety Educator 109

    Chapter 12: Preventing Tragedy 111

    Chapter 13: Hidden 115

    Chapter 14: High 119

    Chapter 15: Hammered 129

    Chapter 16: Mental Health Concerns 139

    Chapter 17: Piecing It All Together 145

About the Author 153

Introduction

I always knew what I wanted to be when I grew up. Ever since I was a little kid, my career path was obvious. I knew I was going to work with sharks. I was going to be a marine biologist working on a boat in the middle of the ocean learning everything about sharks. That is, until I got on a boat and went out into the ocean for the first time and realized how seasick I got. That's when I discovered I was going to have to find another path in life, a plan B, because being a marine biologist who gets seasick just wasn't going to work out for anyone, including the sharks.

When I finished high school, I took the traditional route and went to college. I focused on what every other kid was focusing on – sports. I was recruited to play volleyball and swim for Widener University. Though I attended Widener based on an impulsive decision, it was also where I happened to find myself in my first criminal justice class. In that class, I learned I am a front–and-center-row sitter, and I found myself trying to engage my fellow classmates when my teachers were facilitating lectures and losing everyone's attention.

I was enthralled by the idea of learning about people. I loved watching people, learning about who they are and what they do, and discovering *why* people behave the way they do. I understood the power of body language and how simple facial expressions can influence other people. I was fascinated by people and studied how they responded to behaviors. I went from *watching* all of these behaviors to *studying* them. I had a passion for working with people and helping them. That's when I discovered I was a sociologist at heart.

As I'm sure you've guessed by now, I graduated with degrees in both criminal justice and sociology. After graduating early, I decided to enroll myself in the police academy. I pictured myself wearing my police uniform, helping people in the community, and making their days better. I truly wanted to help, and that's what really drove my spirit.

When I graduated from the police academy in June of 1997, I was fortunate enough to land a department job in August of that same year. This was a very quick turnaround for a police officer candidate to find a job. It wasn't normal, and I realized how lucky I was. I started working for the Lower Gwynedd Police Department, and I've been there ever since, serving in a variety of different roles.

I spent my time on patrol, responding to 911 calls, going out for burglaries and traffic accidents, and taking reports. I quickly learned that policing isn't necessarily about helping people. It isn't always about making people's days better. It's actually a lot of bureaucracy, standardization, red tape, and checkboxes. I was still doing the job to the best of my ability, but I wasn't truly content. Instead of solving problems, I was just a bandage on a wound, a temporary fix to a much larger problem. It wasn't filling the hole in my soul, begging me to do good for others. I felt like I could do more.

Then, one day in 2014, I was off-duty, doing my regular grocery shopping at Wegmans, when my Lieutenant sent me a text message. It said something to the effect of, "Hey, the school district is thinking of starting this program called the School Resource Officer program, and I think it would be a really good fit for you, your personality, and the department. The hours are Monday to Friday, from 7 A.M. to 3 P.M. Are you interested?"

After reading his message, I wrote "YES" in big capital letters, followed by an embarrassing number of exclamation points. This is not an exaggeration. It was far more exclamation points than any grown woman should ever send to her boss in a text message.

The Missing Piece

So…what happens when you desperately want a text message to go through, but you're in a giant warehouse-like building of a grocery store? It doesn't send. My service dropped, and the message wouldn't go through. I was frantically walking around the store, touching the aluminum foil, climbing the shelves with my phone in hand and my arm up in the air, desperately trying to get a signal. I abandoned my cart and ran out of the store. As soon as the text message went through, I went back inside and finished my shopping.

When my Chief called me into his office to discuss the School Resource Officer (SRO) position, he didn't know what it was going to entail. He wasn't going to pin me down with a specific job description, spelling out tasks, responsibilities, and expectations. He trusted my ability to mold the program into something the school district needed and a program I could proudly call my own.

I did exactly that. Ours has since turned into a model program, one that other townships and school districts have used as a guide to building their own. Many districts have since asked me to help them establish their programs, which has been incredibly rewarding! It's an honor to get to work with others who share the same mission I do in bettering our communities through the collaboration between police and our schools. It has also been fun to sculpt this position out of nothing and see how well it has been received.

Being an SRO filled the empty part of my soul that so desperately wanted to help others. My transition into this unique assignment in policing allowed me to support others in a nontraditional way. When you work with kids, every interaction has the potential to make their lives better. This realization shifted my mindset. Instead of trying to solve big-picture problems, I focused on single interactions. I woke up every day determined to make one person's day better as a result of their interaction with me. I still wake up every day with this purpose at heart.

Dr. Beth J. Sanborn

Because I believe so much in what we do, I went back to school for my doctorate to research who SROs are and what we were doing. Just like a sociologist, I wanted to unpack what we, as SROs, do and *why* we do it. I knew we were doing good work, but I wanted to put data behind it so it would resonate with others outside of the SRO community. Even though I'm very active in my SRO network, sometimes you just need hard numbers and an outside perspective.

When I started my research and read what programs were out there, I found one in western Pennsylvania called "Hidden in Plain Sight," which originated in Copely, Ohio. This educational event is a collaborative partnership between the Copely Police Department and Bath Police Department in Pennsylvania, as well as the Ohio Attorney General's Office. The program involved setting up a teenager's mock bedroom with staged furniture and all the other typical items you might find inside their room. Then, organizers sprinkled in a bunch of drug and alcohol paraphernalia around the bedroom. As you go through the room, you begin to uncover different indicators of drug use. This was a valuable educational opportunity, and I saw it as a way to connect with my community's parents.

When I went back to my police station, I told the Chief I wanted to run a similar program in our area. He laughed a little, knowing me and how involved I am. He said, "What? In your spare time?"

Fast forward a few months when the Ambler Branch of Kiwanis, a local philanthropic organization, came to our police department saying they wanted to solve the opioid crisis in our school district. I thought about what a huge undertaking it would be, but how it was also a wonderful idea. I started doing research on my own and digging into the data for our county's Narcan uses. Narcan is the drug used to counteract an opioid overdose. Interestingly enough, I found that even though the opioid crisis was affecting our county, it thankfully wasn't directly impacting the area specific to our school district, which is actually a very small part of our much larger county.

When I say it wasn't affecting our community, I'm not saying there weren't any secondary or tertiary impacts because there likely were, we just didn't know about them. There may have been an extended family member in our immediate community who lost someone to an opioid overdose, but it wasn't a firsthand issue in our schools. When I told the group what I discovered, they then asked me what the issue was in our school district. I simply said, "Marijuana."

That's when my Chief told me to tell the group about this mock teen bedroom I so badly wanted to bring to my community. The group was thrilled with the idea, wanted to support it, and instructed me to make it happen! Although I didn't know it at the time, this exact moment set the ball in motion which ultimately led to the creation and success of my organization Hidden, High, & Hammered.

I started by organizing an event and making it open to the public. An independent company came in and set up the mock teenager's bedroom. I set up a display of stash devices meant to hide drug usage and other poor lifestyle choices for a kid such as vapes, THC, and pills. I coordinated a variety of other vendors to come and set up tables like a health fair, including different services available to kids through the county like Student Assistance Programs, dating violence prevention, family services, drug and alcohol prevention and treatment, mental health prevention and recovery, and suicide prevention information. I thought it was important to have all of these resources present so if a parent had a concern, regardless of what their concern was, there was someone present who could talk to them.

On the evening of the event, I could tell my Chief was thrilled by the turnout. People streamed in and out throughout the entire evening. The auditorium was packed, conversations filled the room, and instructional material was going out in waves. The feedback from our school community was tremendous. My blessing, and curse, is that when I do something, I go over the top. I had it all planned out to down lawn signs to direct people in for parking, balloons to indicate the entrance, food, comment cards, goodie bags for collecting educational materials, and pencils left out for people to take notes and leave comments. I even had news coverage there. My Chief was impressed, if I do say so myself.

It seriously just started with a mock teen bedroom – that was it. I did a few more events in that style, and then it transformed into a health-fair-style event with other ancillary-type services. After doing that, I discovered other police jurisdictions were doing these mock teen bedrooms as well, but no one else had the additional service providers there like I did. The way I was doing it was unique in and of itself. This is when I knew I was onto something!

It went from a mock teen bedroom event hosted by SRO Sanborn under the authority of the Lower Gwynedd Police Department, to developing my own program and company called Hidden, High, & Hammered LLC, presented by Detective Dr. Beth J. Sanborn. My mission is to help parents, teachers, and social services providers learn indicators of poor lifestyle choices among students so, together, we can identify a student who may be in crisis and intervene before that crisis is reached.

Then, through the course of being in schools, I noticed how students weren't just hiding drugs, but the drugs themselves started to look different. I adapted "hidden" from hiding drugs and "high" from the drugs themselves. One morning, a student chugged a can of beer right in the middle of the school library. Friends took pictures and videos and put them on Instagram. When I wanted to come up with another word that began with an

The Missing Piece

H to talk about students drinking and experimenting with alcohol, my fourteen-year-old daughter said, "Hammered."

That's how the name Hidden, High, & Hammered was born.

On top of the drug and alcohol experimentation, I was seeing an extraordinary number of mental health concerns in students. Whether they were experimenting with drugs as a way to self-medicate or cope with self-diagnosed depression or anxiety, it was a way to make themselves feel better in the moment. Through this self-medication, they were looking to solve their problems on their own, but they couldn't figure out how to solve them in a healthy way. I added the communication piece to my program because I found it was important for all stakeholders to be involved in a child's life. Parents, teachers, coaches, principals, and community members all needed to be at the table to encourage healthy coping mechanisms and positive lifestyle choices.

In the back of my mind, I was thinking about the school shooting at Arapahoe High School in 2013, which took the life of Claire Davis. Following that tragedy, the Davis family brought all of the invested stakeholders in the shooter's life to share the information they had. Individually, the pieces of information each of them had meant little or nothing. But when they put all of those pieces together, the picture of a student who was in crisis became clear. As I added mental health and communication as integral pieces to my program, all of the puzzle pieces came together to create the mission of Hidden, High, & Hammered.

SRO Sanborn to Detective Dr. Beth Sanborn, sole proprietor, was an evolution that took place over the course of three or four years. It came from identifying a need and studying these trends in the school. There's no denying that drug use has evolved faster than ever before. Vaping and THC oils didn't even exist when I assumed the role of SRO seven years ago. They're a new beast, and drug and alcohol companies are specifically targeting our kids. Because of my relationships and experience working with students, I've been able to offer a perspective a lot of parents don't get. I mean, really, as a parent, how much would you be willing to pay to watch your kids in their own environment when they don't see you or know you're there?

The funny thing is, despite being in a police uniform, students often talk openly to each other right in front of me. Much like the janitor from *Sixteen Candles*, I see and hear it all! That's what I get to do every day when I enter the school building. In fact, it's my job. As an SRO, I interact with students in an environment where they feel comfortable on their own "home turf." I watch them interact with their friends, exercise their independence, and observe their evolution as they figure out who they want to be. Over time, I watch them mature and discover their identities. I also get to encourage their development as I cheer them on to make smart choices and think about their future.

I have a unique perspective on each student, and my perspective may not be the same as their teachers', coaches', or parents' view of them. Because of this, I'm able to talk to parents and let them know what their children are doing, how they're acting and behaving, and what language they use when their parents aren't around. No, I'm not tattling on anyone, but I am sharing my unique piece of information because I get to see the personalities the students are exhibiting to their peers when they think no one is watching.

The belief that I'm only there to arrest students is one of the biggest misconceptions about my role as an SRO. In actuality, I am so much more than that. As an SRO, I have three essential functions, which aren't ranked in any particular order. The best part about it is I can focus as much or as little on any one of these three functions as is needed by my school district or community. These focuses can change on a daily basis or from school to school, and an SRO has the autonomy to adjust as needed.

The Missing Piece

One of the three functions is law enforcement. This means I wear a traditional police uniform, drive a marked police car parked in front of the school, and carry a full complement of tools on my duty belt. Though SROs have the option to wear a more informal uniform of cargo pants and a polo shirt, my decision to wear a formal uniform is intentional. My chief and I decided very early on that we didn't want the students to confuse me with any other role like a security guard, a custodian, a secretary, or even a teacher. The police administration wanted it to be very clear and establish I am a police officer. This way, in an emergency or crisis, there would be no confusion as to who I am. All of the kids from elementary school through high school and beyond recognize me wearing the same clothes as what they are taught to look for in a community helper from day one. That's me. Officer Beth!

My second function is that of an informal counselor/mentor, which means I am trained to be able to talk to a student in an age and developmentally appropriate language, de-escalate situations, be an active listener, participate in conversations, and learn how to make people feel seen and heard. I do all of this so I can be a positive role model for them. All too often, the general public's interactions with law enforcement are momentary. They happen when you're in crisis, possibly at the lowest point of your life, or even when you're not in a mindset where you're receptive to conversation. One of the best parts about my job is that I have the luxury of time with students. I have the opportunity to work with kids over the course of 180 days in just one school year. When I say "work with," I really emphasize the *with*.

Kids sometimes do dumb things, let's be real here. They do something silly or make a mistake because they weren't thinking or because their brains just aren't fully developed yet to know better. When they make that mistake, I could read them their rights and spend five minutes taking law enforcement actions. I could write them a ticket or assess a fine and arrest them depending on the severity of the infraction.

But again, that's not what I do. Instead, using the luxury of time, I can work with that kid tomorrow, the next day, and the day after that to figure out why they're engaged in that behavior to begin with. I ask questions to challenge their thinking. What were you trying to achieve or accomplish? Do you still think doing that is a good idea? I am trained to look at the "why" behind a student's behaviors. I turn their mistakes into teachable moments because that's what a positive role model does, especially in a school environment, which is designed for learning. Remember, SROs are in school to enhance and supplement the learning environment, not detract from it. The fun part is that each of those interactions, over time, can be casual and brief. They don't have to be formal sessions. Sometimes a quick check-in or an acknowledgment and a smile can go a long way.

My third essential function is to act as a public safety educator. Now, I'm not walking into a chemistry class and running a lab experiment, but I can walk into a classroom when they're talking about the Constitution and educate students on their rights. I can go into a driver's education class and talk about how to safely operate a vehicle or what to do when you get pulled over by the police. I can walk into a health class and talk about vaping, sexting, social media, and proper digital citizenship. I can teach lessons that have real-world implications and applications.

Because teaching is an essential part of my responsibilities, it's my job to recognize a need and then address it. I am responsible for the safety, well-being, health, development, and sustainability of my school. That's not just for students; it's for staff, administration, parents, and anyone else associated with the school community. If a student experiences a crisis, the effects of that crisis impact more than just the student themselves. If a student harms themselves, that harm creates a ripple effect of trauma, spreading it out through a much wider range. I teach people to prevent the crisis so their friends, family members, acquaintances, and community don't ever have to mourn, endure a negative milestone, or have to remember the pain or loss.

18

The Missing Piece

When I identify a concern, like the long-term consequences of unidentified drug and alcohol use or the evolution of drugs, I see it as my responsibility to educate the stakeholders. By educating everyone involved, we can strengthen the safety net we have worked so hard to create for our children. These kids are OUR kids. I am just as invested in the success of our kids and our communities, so I treat all of them as if they were my own.

These three essential functions of law enforcement, informal counselor/mentor, and public safety educator make up the "SRO Triad," as it's called by the National Association of School Resource Officers (NASRO).

Parents, educators, and anyone who interacts regularly with children – this book is for you. Get to know your School Resource Officer. Regardless of your preconceived notions of police officers, trained SROs are on your team. If your child appears to be struggling or is experiencing a sudden change in behavior, talk to your SRO just like you might the school counselor or their teacher. Our job is to see things others may not notice or think twice about. We are trained to support your children. We might even have the missing piece of the puzzle you call your child.

Part I: Law Enforcement

Of the three major functions of an SRO, this one might not come as a surprise. SROs are, in fact, law enforcement professionals. What we do is highly specialized because we are in a more controlled environment working with a vulnerable population. The specific skills and duties we may need to employ on any given day vary greatly from those of our colleagues out walking the beat, but that is part of what makes it so rewarding and one of the reasons I fell in love with the role.

In addition to learning more about the specific job description of the SRO assigned to your child's school, I want all parents to gain insight into how juvenile law differs from adult law, the human element we bring into the halls, and the many ways we help to bridge the gap between cops and kids.

Chapter 1: SRO 101

Based on the federal definition, a school resource officer (SRO) is a sworn police officer who is hired by a municipality and assigned to work in conjunction with the school district. I am stationed inside our school district, so I like to consider my schools as my patrol beat.

There are a lot of misconceptions about who an SRO is, what we do, and what our roles are. You know the stereotype of that cop with mirrored sunglasses, arms folded across his chest, and intimidating body language? We are all familiar with the anxiety and fear of getting pulled over and seeing that cop strutting towards your car – including me! The first time seeing a uniformed officer with a full duty belt in your child's school can seem unnecessary and unsettling. But those intimidating figures wearing mirrored sunglasses are not who SROs are. In fact, we're quite the opposite.

Doctors can be podiatrists, proctologists, brain surgeons, chiropractors, psychiatrists, dentists, or professors. Each of these jobs is very different, but the person doing them all carries the title of doctor. Just like doctors, police officers also have specialties, and not every officer is meant for every specialty. A K9 officer might not be a good hostage negotiator, and a vice detective might not be a good school resource officer.

As a law enforcement officer, my boss falls within the hierarchy of the police department, so I report directly to my Lieutenant and Chief of Police. However, in a school building, the principal is the Chief. Even before stepping foot into the school building, there has to be a very clearly defined memorandum of understanding (MOU), a contractual agreement, so anyone who reads the agreement would understand what my role is as an outsider or a third-party contractor. Otherwise, there could be a misconception that the SRO is merely there for security, or worse yet, as the cop who gives students detention for running in the hallway or who is there proactively to arrest children. That's *not* what we do, so the MOU clearly spells that out.

Even though the principal is not the boss, that doesn't give SROs any reason to disrespect the principal's position. If you're an outsider in the building and the principal doesn't like you, doesn't understand your role, or doesn't think you can support their school environment, there's a good chance the principal is going to get you removed from their building.

This is one reason SROs work really hard to make their principals happy. We still bend over backward to ensure we are communicating with them and that their ideology for how they want to run their school is evident in our actions. Basically, we want to make sure we are trying to achieve the same goals within the school while approaching them from two different directions. SROs are there to enhance the learning environment, not detract from it. We want students to feel safe and secure, so they have fewer distractions getting in the way of learning.

Working formally under the police department and informally under the schools can sometimes be tricky. It's a constant balancing act. The police department will always say I'm first and foremost a police officer. While they're not wrong, I also have discretion. A few years ago, we were having a lot of fights at one of my schools. When I returned to the station day after day, exhausted and frustrated, my Chief's question was, "Why aren't you locking them all up?"

If I did that, there wouldn't be anyone in school the next day. There wouldn't be any fights, but there also wouldn't be any education happening either. That's not necessarily the right way to respond to your boss, but there are many different interventions we can take before arresting a child. Sometimes, an outside officer will hear about a fight in school, which is considered assault in law enforcement, and their natural response is to effectuate an arrest. An SRO, on the other hand,

24

recognizes the need to look at the totality of the circumstances. We need to look at the "why" behind the behavior and understand why a fight may have occurred. If we decide to make an arrest, we should be able to explain why an arrest is necessary and how it solves the problem and prevents it from recurring.

I will state this many times throughout this book, but I want to say it early on – an arrest is rarely our first response to interactions with students. I've been caught in the middle of many unpleasant circumstances. I have to have these conversations regularly to explain what the role of an SRO is and how, even though I do have the power to arrest, it's not always the right option to employ. Simply because a crime occurred does not mean we need to make an arrest.

A few years ago, there was a girl who was struggling with mental health issues that caused her to become aggressive at school and at home. Her mom called the police one night because her daughter was in her bedroom with a butcher knife, and she was screaming and cursing, threatening the family. In policing, this is a bad combination that has the potential for a bad outcome. Thankfully, there was a good outcome in this case, and she was on the path to getting the help she needed. When I got back to school, the administration and her guidance counselor heard about what happened. They asked me why I didn't lock her up.

I challenged them by asking, "What good would that do?"

An arrest doesn't mean she is going to get packed up and shipped away to a mysterious land where no one would ever see her again. Instead, it might mean she gets a yellow copy of a ticket and is told to appear at the courthouse down the street at some date a few weeks from now for her court hearing. Then, she'd be back in school the next day after she got her ticket. An arrest won't calm a mental health crisis. Appearing in front of a judge won't cure mental illness. But care, treatment, supervision, and other services just might, and I am able to make those referrals for parents and students.

Dr. Beth J. Sanborn

Of the three facets of my job, I most strongly identify with the informal counselor/mentor role. In the course of my duties, I do very little active law enforcement and formal teaching, but I spend most of my time mentoring and counseling. I make it a point of being observant at all times. If I see a kid in the hallway who suddenly looks like they are going to burst into tears, I will gently approach them and offer to take them to a safe place where their classmates won't see them cry. I will invite them into my office, offer them a seat, and get them some tissues and a bottle of water. I will tell them to take a minute and breathe. Sometimes they want to talk and sometimes they would rather sit in silence. I'm there to offer them whatever they need at that moment.

That's the role of mentoring and counseling. Is that traditional police work? No. Yet, that is how I spend much of my day. I talk with students all day long because communication is an essential part of building relationships and trust. We might talk about a poor grade they received, a tumultuous relationship, or excitement for an upcoming sporting event. Conversations can range from simply sharing a moment of pride about receiving their driver's permit or can be as serious as the first disclosure of molestation and abuse. None of these conversations would occur without the students' trust.

This is where I find I am able to excel. By being observant and building relationships with students, they trust me enough to come to talk to me when they're in crisis. Yes, there are guidance counselors and crisis counselors whom students can speak with. But without a foundation of trust, they may not feel comfortable speaking to an adult about a crisis for the first time. Without those small, casual, positive interactions, I worry students may not disclose a very serious concern because they don't feel they have a safe connection with any adult when they are ready to have that conversation. As my daughter so eloquently suggested to me, "Talk to kids casually when you can so it makes it easier when you have to talk with them seriously."

The Missing Piece

I have had a number of kids come to me and say, "Officer Beth, I can't talk to my guidance counselor." The guidance counselor is there for guidance, but the guidance counselor also has a full stack of student caseloads. They have to help with students' course selections and college recommendations. They have a million things they have to do for 500 students, whereas I have the flexibility to be able to talk with anyone and everyone at any time. As I help one student, I find they vouch for me with their peers. Students have often come to me saying their friends encouraged them to come to talk with me.

Over the course of my career, I've taken my fair share of disclosures from students. Sometimes they are firsthand disclosures of sexual abuse, physical abuse, neglect, or trauma that nobody has ever heard before. But, to be clear, that doesn't just happen on the first day of school at 7 A.M. It happens over time, as we build those relationships, as they see me every day and know I'm going to smile, and as I often overlook their minor infractions.

Let me clarify what I mean by overlooking minor infractions. If I see a student walking through the hallway eating a hoagie and they look at me with the most guilty look on their face I have ever seen in my life, I will smile and ask, "What's for lunch today?"

They might respond, "Turkey and cheese."

To which I will say, "Sounds good," and keep walking.

I'm not going to send that kid to the Assistant Principal or kick them back into the cafeteria. More often than not, I'm just going to nicely ask them to do me a favor and clean up their trash. Don't make it look like you were eating and walking through the hallways. Small interactions like these build so much credibility and trust because I interact with students like they're real people.

Is walking through the halls eating a violation of a school rule? In my school, it is. But I am not a disciplinarian or an enforcer of

27

school rules. I am not there to turn the school environment into a police state. I am there to build relationships, be a positive role model, and keep kids safe. When I walk down the hallways, I tend to make a lot of noise with the clinking and clanking of keys and equipment on my toolbelt. If I see a bunch of students standing around in a huddle, I'll ask, lightheartedly and with a smile, "What did I catch y'all doing?"

They usually say they weren't doing anything, even though they look at me wide-eyed and frozen. I laugh and tell them their faces say otherwise. Then, I tell them to get back to class and that's it. They walk one way, and I intentionally walk the other way. Those teeny-tiny interactions may seem insignificant, but they build trust and credibility by letting them know I am not trying to trap them or get them in trouble. Instead, I want them to know I will be here for them if they are in crisis, that I'm around, and I'm looking out for them. These interactions are the heart of my role as an SRO. Investing in the community, treating people with respect, knowing what is needed in the moment, and then delivering it – that's my job. And I absolutely love my job.

In order for an SRO to be successful, there needs to be a program in place for them to thrive. A good SRO program requires properly selecting, training, and equipping an SRO for your school. You don't want to have that stereotypical cop with sunglasses and folded arms, swinging a baton and smacking it against the lockers, asking your kids where their hall pass is, or arresting them for stealing a pack of Oreos from the cafeteria. That doesn't do anyone any good. In fact, it can do more harm than good. This is why you need to have someone who is properly selected and properly trained, someone who wants to do the job and is doing it for the right reasons.

You need someone who can take ownership of these kids and treat them as their own, someone who wants them to succeed, and someone who genuinely enjoys working with children. Being a police officer in a school environment is very different from patrolling the mean streets of wherever you are. A school environment is meant to be safe and protected so it can provide a nurturing learning environment for students. An SRO should always work toward strengthening the educational environment. Kids should feel comfortable enough to learn, build relationships, grow into themselves, and discover who they are.

Part of an SRO's training is learning about child development during adolescence, the science of the teenage brain, de-escalation tactics, and communication skills. Being properly trained means being able to look at a situation from the three different perspectives of the SRO triad: law enforcement, informal counselor/mentor, and public safety educator. The majority of our training is rooted in this triad and in understanding the significance of each of these three roles.

In addition to these roles, we are also trained in ethics. When you work with such a vulnerable population, it isn't enough to just act ethically, you have to give the appearance of acting ethically as well. That may sound strange, so let me give you an example.

Let's say an SRO at your school is married to the math teacher at the same school. If that police officer goes into the math teacher's classroom and closes the door, you might think there are some shenanigans afoot, right? They may simply be having lunch together or discussing a student, but it's the perception of something going on that could be perceived as unethical. Anytime you are working with kids, you are put under a microscope. It's not enough to act ethically, you have to appear ethical in everything you do.

Aside from all the hard skills we learn in policing such as emergency vehicle driving, defensive tactics, and firearms training, SROs have to learn soft skills. Two of the most important soft skills for SROs are effective communication and active listening. It's learning how to talk to elementary school kids differently than high school seniors. You can't talk to the principal the same way you would the superintendent, the media, a parent, or your police chief. Each of these people needs to be spoken to

Dr. Beth J. Sanborn

in a different manner, so you need to learn multiple communication styles. You have to be able to express your meaning, so the recipient fully understands the message conveyed.

The other major part of our job is active listening. We need to be able to clearly hear what kids are telling us, to ask clarifying questions, and make sure we understand what we're being told. This also applies to our interactions with teachers and school staff. We need to be able to listen to multiple perspectives so we can put all of those pieces together and understand a situation. If we don't understand, we need to take ownership of that and ask questions. For example, it's okay to ask for clarification when a slang term is used. If someone refers to a stick, it could mean anything from a shotgun to a cigar, to a skinny person, or a piece of wood from a tree. It all depends on the context. Rather than assuming its meaning and potentially assuming wrong, asking clarifying questions allows us to communicate properly.

We are also trained in how to work with diverse groups of students. The focus is not just on racial diversities but includes cultural, linguistic, physical, learning, and even neurodiversities. We have an opportunity to work with students in marginalized groups in schools and also interact and speak with them in their own environment. We encounter students with special needs in schools more so than police officers would out on the streets. It's just as important for us to learn to interact with them as it is for them to learn to interact with us, especially because some of these children may never encounter police officers outside of their school environment. We get to build relationships with these students and teach them how to build relationships with us because school is a learning environment.

Some of my favorite encounters have included a student telling me about a traditional Thai dress she was planning to wear to prom or being asked to walk around the track with one of the special education students during his breaks because he was fascinated by police officers and wanted to be my partner. These simple interactions made the kids smile, which, in turn, made me smile. My biggest smile came a few years ago from a student when I finally pronounced his name properly. Knowing students' names and being able to pronounce them correctly is a small but huge aspect of building relationships. I had been trying, and he politely corrected me a few times. I will never forget the smile on his face once I finally got it right. I used it every time we spoke after that, and he smiled just as big every time.

Other areas of training focus on violence and victimization. Students come from all different backgrounds, some of which may be very different from our own, so we learn about adverse childhood experiences (ACEs) and how they can negatively impact students' ability to learn or behave according to our expectations. We are taught to understand the cycle of victimization and how students who are abused or neglected at home may become victims of bullying or socially withdraw from their peers. We are taught that students may perceive interactions differently, that something seemingly innocuous could be a trigger, and that behavior can be unpredictable. Learning how to manage the unpredictable can be one of the hardest skills to master, but it's necessary when working with children. Not only is behavior unpredictable from one student to another, but the same student may react unpredictably from day to day or from encounter to encounter.

Then, of course, we learn about the law, what we're allowed to do, and what we shouldn't be doing. We learn about protecting ourselves from liability and protecting the rights of students. We look at Constitutional law and how it can be interpreted when working with children. Though the laws regarding children sometimes give schools more leeway, it doesn't mean we should take advantage of that. If a police officer wants to search for something, they need probable cause, which means there is a probability a crime occurred and this person had suspected involvement in the crime. However, in 1985, New Jersey v. T.L.O. was a landmark court case that lessens the standards required for police officers in schools to be able to search. In order for

Dr. Beth J. Sanborn

T.L.O. protections to be applied, the search has to be reasonable in its scope and justified in its inception. If those two prongs are met, then instead of requiring probable cause, the officer only needs reasonable suspicion, which is a lower threshold.

In other words, as a police officer who is an established part of the school community (an SRO), I can search based on reasonable suspicion as opposed to probable cause. However, if my partner, who is out on street patrol, comes into the school, he can only search by probable cause, not reasonable suspicion. Just because you *can* do something doesn't mean you *should*. When you're working with kids, you always want to make sure you're going above and beyond to protect them. We don't want to take advantage of their age, their mindset, their development, or their language by searching students or their belongings simply because we can.

In addition to all of these important laws and distinctions when working with students, we learn threat response, school safety, emergency operations planning, and how to collaborate with schools to achieve these safety measures. There's often a misconception that police officers are just big, dumb, brute cops, but SROs are specially trained to work in an educational environment.

If I'm going to do a job, I want to do it to the best of my abilities. I want to make sure I'm serving my kids because they are going to grow up and be adults in my community. We have the ability to set the tone for how kids and families perceive police officers as a whole. Once families leave the school setting, we want them to remember the positive interactions and have good experiences to share with others. These relationships are important in the moment and create a ripple effect that lasts long into the future.

Aside from being properly selected and properly trained, SROs also need to be properly equipped because it's really difficult to do your job when you don't have the proper tools. If you're working in a school environment, there are a lot of different things you might need to make your job easier, like an office or a private place where you can safely talk to a child who trusts you or wants to disclose personal information. Although you don't *need* to have this, it's much more comfortable for a child to speak with you in a private spot instead of in the middle of a cafeteria with 300 sets of eyes and ears on them.

You also need to have the ability for people to contact you. I'm very fortunate my school district has given me a ton of different tools to establish myself as a member of our school community. I have an office, a laptop, a cell phone, a school ID card, a lunch account, and my picture in the yearbook. I participate in the school community and get involved so I can learn about the culture of the building and the subcultures within. I've learned an awful lot about working with teenagers and preteens, which I might not have known otherwise if I hadn't become more involved in the school community.

Properly selected, trained, and equipped SROs can make all the difference in keeping the schools and the community safe. If you, as a parent, think an SRO program would benefit your school and community, I encourage you to speak with your school board, your principal, and your local police department. Inquire about the possibility of starting this program in your schools as another resource to help students and families.

If an SRO program is something you see value in, speak with other parents too. Parents have tremendous input into decisions made in schools. When coming together, minivan moms are a powerful force. If they understand the SRO position and the different roles SROs serve, they can advocate for it. Special action groups get things done. There are few groups more passionate than parents working toward setting their children up for success. If parents can work together to support the same goal, your school administration, your local police department, and your community will hear you.

Chapter 2: Policing Through a Different Lens

Within juvenile law, my role is still to be a police officer. I have arrested kids, but it's not my first, go-to response. I always try at least a half dozen other interventions before it gets to an arrest, but there are some circumstances out of my control that require me to make an arrest.

Before I assumed the role of SRO, I had been on patrol for 18 years. I knew Pennsylvania criminal law, the rules of criminal procedure, and how to safely and procedurally police in the adult arena. Trust me when I say working with children is an entirely different ball game. There is a completely different set of skills needed to effectively work with children, and there is a set of laws made specifically for juveniles.

Juveniles have extra protections under the law, and it's important to understand those distinctions. The language is different, the players are different, and the goals are different. The goal of the juvenile justice system is to maintain the family unit through treatment, supervision, and rehabilitation. In the juvenile system, we don't use terms like "offenders" or "defendants" as we do with adults because we don't want to stigmatize children. The goal is not to arrest them but to help them learn from their mistakes.

When I started as an SRO, I had to relearn juvenile law. I had to learn the processes, procedures, and paperwork. Most importantly, I had to fully understand the mindset behind this type of law. When talking about children, I often say, "Kids do dumb stuff. Let's face it – they're kids, and sometimes they do dumb stuff." I don't mean this in an offensive way at all. Children make mistakes, no matter how smart they are, because their brains are still developing and they're still learning.

Well, sometimes based on the circumstances of that dumb thing, police may need to get involved and legal action may need to be taken. However, this doesn't necessarily mean the child needs to be entered into the juvenile justice system. As I'm sure you can imagine, the juvenile justice system will more than likely create hurdles and roadblocks in a kid's future and might irreparably derail a child from being successful.

In doing my research on juvenile programs, I found the Youth Aid Panel, which is sponsored and run by the District Attorney's office. It's designed as a diversion from the criminal justice system, giving children a second chance after "doing dumb stuff." Sometimes the Youth Aid Panel is jokingly referred to as kiddie community service. The program panel is made up of a bunch of invested stakeholders in the community like parents and business owners. There are no cops, no lawyers, and no judges. It's made up of people who truly want to see kids succeed despite the mistakes they might have made. The Youth Aid Panel members believe in children, and they believe every child can be successful even after they do something dumb and make a mistake.

So, if a child does something dumb and commits an act that falls under the purview of the panel, the child can accept responsibility for it, admit it wasn't the best choice to make, and declare they aren't going to do it again. If they take ownership of their behavior, they can be rewarded by being diverted away from the juvenile justice system. Instead, they are sent to do community service. The interesting part about this program is the panel treats each kid individually. If you have a child who is terrified of horses, their community service wouldn't be mucking stalls at the horse stable. That will only set them up for failure. The end result is intended to be a win for the child and a win for the community. When you have a child do something they love or feel passionate about, they take accountability for their mistakes while also doing good for others. If a child likes reading, they might have to dedicate a certain number of hours to volunteering at a homework club or reshelving books at the library.

The Missing Piece

One of my students, who was struggling with behavior issues, really liked skateboarding. He also mentioned he might be interested in engineering or design. When I referred him to the Youth Aid Panel after a violation, I suggested to his panel liaison to have him design a skate park. He had to draw it and do calculations to determine proper measurements for various skate jumps. He really enjoyed doing that because it made him think about what he loved and how he could create a flow for a skate park. Although a local skate park already existed, it afforded him the opportunity to consider its design and learn a lot in the process.

The Youth Aid Panel program is phenomenal because it accomplishes a couple of goals. It serves the community by encouraging kids to become invested in it, and it supports them to try something new in an area they already have an interest in. It's not just a rubber stamp program to show accountability for your actions – it's a win-win all around. In Montgomery County, Pennsylvania in 2019, the Youth Aid Panel program referred 489 youths who performed a total of 2,304 hours of community service. They had a 93.6% completion rate and a 3.5% recidivism rate. They collected $5,835 in restitution. There were 260 panel volunteers, 38 monthly meetings on average, and 33 referring police departments.

I've been a huge proponent of the Youth Aid Panel because I believe in diversion. Not every dumb choice needs to result in criminalization. This belief is popular among SROs because we're invested in our communities and want to see children succeed. While I can't sit on the panel because it goes against the whole concept of not having law enforcement involved, I've made it my mission to learn everything there is to know about what the program entails and how it operates.

As a law enforcement officer, I can help advocate for children by recommending them to the panel. I have to really know a kid and understand their heart and mind in order to make that recommendation, but it's an incredible opportunity to divert kids away from the juvenile justice system and give them a second chance. I take what I do seriously and am thankful to be in a position that allows me to make a positive impact in the lives of our children. After all, they are the future of our communities.

Child Advocacy Centers and their forensic interviewers are other resources for juveniles. Mission Kids Child Advocacy Center is the child advocacy center in my area. People who work at these centers are trained to talk to children who are victims or witnesses to crimes. They have expertise in speaking to children in an age-appropriate manner, which allows each child to speak their truth and use their voice to promote healing.

What I find to be amazing about the child advocacy center model is children only have to share a story one time. For a moment, imagine being a child who has been victimized. You may tell your mom your story for the first time, then your mom takes you to the police station, and you have to tell the story again to the police officer. Then a detective interviews you, and you have to tell the story again. Then maybe a doctor gets involved, and you find yourself having to tell this story for the fourth time. After that, you have to tell the story to the attorney who is taking the case, who then has to take you through witness prep, so you can share your story again in court. At this point, you've had to recall this traumatic event and share your story at least seven times. You've had to relive the worst moment of your life over and over again, bringing yourself right back to the instance where you can see, hear, smell, and feel everything you somatically experienced.

Having to relive a traumatic experience as an adult is painful, so imagine the effects it can have on a child. Imagine I asked you, a grown adult, to explain to me in detail your last sexual encounter. You'd probably look at me blankly, then laugh uncomfortably. You might even tell me to mind my own business. Even if it were pleasant and consensual, you would probably feel awkward sharing the details with a total stranger, and you might even need some prompting to share. Now imagine if you were a child and the encounter wasn't consensual. You might feel guilt, shame, fear, or a combination of all of those. As that child, would you want to relive the worst day of your life over and over again?

In these forensic interviews, a child only has to tell their story one time. They're in a safe environment, not an interrogation room at the precinct. This room is small and cozy with plush furniture. When they meet the forensic interviewer, they are told the room has cameras and microphones and there is a whole team of people in the other room who are watching them and want to help. This team is composed of a combination of important players in the juvenile justice system, including a police officer, family advocate, attorney, and detective. Everyone is there to advocate for children and evaluate the situation objectively. The professionals watch so they can all get the information from a single interview. This way the child doesn't have to keep repeating their story over and over again.

This multidisciplinary team approach allows us to talk about and brainstorm how to best support the child. Oftentimes, if a young child who has been victimized is not cared for properly, this can start the cycle of victimization, making it more likely for the victim to become the victimizer. This is the whole snowball effect. I'm a big supporter of Mission Kids because their procedures and protocols are designed to minimize trauma, support children to become healthy adults, and end the cycles of violence and victimization. Their mission is close to my heart, so I volunteer with them as one of their multidisciplinary team members.

My first juvenile case was a young girl who was molested by her uncle. As I was investigating, I learned the actual incident occurred outside of my jurisdiction, which meant it wasn't my case to investigate. I took all the work I had done up to that point, wrapped it all nice and neat with a bow, and handed it over to the other detective who was going to be handling it. Her uncle had taken off across the country, but detectives successfully got a warrant and brought him back. He went to trial, was convicted, and was sentenced. I was so proud of this girl that I went to her house after the case had ended with a gift card for Rita's Italian

Ice. I told her what a great job she did. She was so excited to see me, she introduced me to her hamster, and everything seemed great.

Fast forward a few years, and she started coming across my radar regularly due to sexual activity and sexual aggression. This sweet, little girl, who I was proud of for being so brave in court, now had her name coming across my desk more and more often on the wrong side of the law. I was frustrated and angry, but it wasn't her fault. It's not unusual or unexpected for a victim to later become a victimizer, no matter how cared for they are in the process, but helping them to deal with childhood trauma lessens the likelihood of victims acting out. Things could have actually been worse in this scenario, but they still weren't great.

She has since been identified as an offender in numerous cases. To some extent, I have had to learn to balance my feelings and recognize she is now victimizing others. She is creating new criminal cases. It's difficult to see the cycle, and I wish I could break it for her. I still interact with this family regularly, and it's not easy. These kids are still teenagers, and I often worry about whom they are going to become as adults. I work really hard to break this cycle for children like her while also protecting other kids from becoming her victims.

It's incredibly important for SROs to take inventory of the resources in their community that serve the juvenile justice system. I found the programs in my area through conversations and relationship-building with other youth advocates in my network. It's our job to know what's available in our communities. They can vary regionally, and there may even be some that support kids in specific circumstances. It's important to know who does what in your county and state. Even knowing what business owners contribute to charities is important because you never know who might be hosting an open gym where kids can go after school to burn off steam. There may be a custodian who repurposes bicycles and provides them to kids in the community, the local community cupboard may provide food, clothing, and cleaning supplies to families, or a local philanthropist may be willing to write a check if you explain the need to make a specific purchase. You'd be surprised by the number of community-minded people and organizations so I can't stress enough the importance of knowing what resources are available in your community.

The fact that one of the roles of law enforcement is to make arrests is the driving force behind those who are against having police officers in schools. People assume making arrests is our sole function and the only reason we are there. Imagine your knee hurts and you go to a doctor. The doctor isn't going to immediately recommend knee surgery. First, he's going to recommend resting it or taking it easy. If that doesn't work, he may suggest taking some over-the-counter pain medicine and trying some ice. Then he may say to try elevating it. If none of that works over a period of time, he may refer you to physical therapy or even a specialist, who is going to run tests and scans and try new healing measures. Finally, if all else fails, and the only option left is surgery, then it may be considered.

As police officers, we respond in a similar way. We don't immediately jump to the highest level of intervention, which would be an arrest. There are so many different steps we can take to intervene, and we have the discretion to use these as we see fit. If there is a kid who is constantly truant and the school is responding the same way over and over again with no success, an SRO can look at the same problem through a different lens and offer a different solution.

This is why I often refer to the role of an SRO as policing through a different lens. We aren't there to be a big, bad cop, demanding order and arresting bad guys. These are children. They don't necessarily need to be arrested. As long as they aren't causing injury or destruction in a way that threatens the safety of themselves or others, arresting them is not going to be my first intervention. Oftentimes, this behavior is merely a child crying out for help or attention, and what they really need is a shoulder to

41

lean on or to feel heard. Because many children don't know how to communicate how they are feeling, they express it through their behaviors, which can sometimes be challenging for adults. But we have to remember that's how they show us they need something, and most often, they need love.

That being said, if there is an assault in my school and a kid winds up in the hospital with a broken bone and has a parent there looking for answers, I have to investigate and compile information to determine what happened and how this incident occurred. Victims have a tremendous amount of impact on how incidents are handled, and there are a lot of pieces to consider when determining whether or not an arrest is going to be made. We look at both the victim and the offender, as well as the circumstances, video footage, witness statements, witness reliability, and any other information we have. Ultimately, the victim and their family tend to have a lot of influence over that.

The ultimate decision as to what charges are pursued or not is in the hands of the District Attorney (DA)'s Office, but those decisions are not made lightly or even by one person. It's a collaborative decision oftentimes with the investigator, the family, and the DA. It's dependent on what the act is, whether it is a clear-cut case planned ahead of time, and if there were injuries involved. There's little room for error. Although the attorneys want to argue over every area for potential loopholes, there's little room for these arguments until the case gets taken to court.

If there's an instance where a child has forewarned his friends to stand around with their cell phones, ready to capture every angle on video, it's clear they were planning an attack. When another kid is walking through the cafeteria with his lunch tray and gets blindsided by this attack and everyone is filming it, it's very clear it was premeditated. Then you have to consider if there was intent to cause bodily harm or injury and if it was meant to be a spectacle. In cases like these, there's even less room for argument.

The Missing Piece

If there's no prior conflict, the kids are frenemies (sometimes friends, sometimes enemies), and the parents agree to handle it with the understanding that sometimes kids will be kids, then I don't force myself into the situation. I would never force a child to be a victim in the criminal justice process and then criminalize the offender, especially when that's not what the family wants. Sometimes, a family does want there to be accountability though, so it's not black and white. The mere presence of criminal activity doesn't necessarily result in an arrest. There are so many more variables taken into consideration.

But here's the thing, if I make an arrest, it's more than likely a child I've met before because they're one of my students. I know them, and I talk to them by name. I've established a reputation, so they know who I am. They know I'm going to treat them with respect, and I'm not going to lie to them. I'm not going to sneak up on them or show up at their house dressed in SWAT gear, kick down the front door, and arrest them while they're eating dinner on the sofa. Instead, I'm going to talk them through what's going to happen. When you surprise someone or catch them off-guard, their response is much less predictable. Removing the uncertainty and the unknown keeps everyone much safer, myself included. You can de-escalate and calm people down when they know what to expect.

If a kid messes up, like really messes up to the point where I might not be able to help them out of it, I'll have that conversation with them. I will say, "Look, this investigation is coming to me. You now made me act like Officer Beth. I'm going to walk you through exactly what is going to happen. I'm going to help you through this. Just like I love you and want to protect you, I also have to protect the other kids I love as well."

I can only think of a single instance when I had to put a kid in handcuffs in the school building. Contrary to what many people think, we aren't perp walking kids in handcuffs through the cafeteria to show off our authority. As a police officer, that does nothing to establish credibility with students. We are already wearing a police uniform, and the students know who we are, so there's no need to assert our dominance. If I do have to arrest a student, it is usually procedural and involves paperwork, and the arrest is made outside of school or discretely away from the masses.

Because this line is blurry, let me give an example of needing to perform law enforcement duties, without needing to make an arrest. It had been brought to my attention that a teacher witnessed a student searching the internet about weapons and ballistic materials on a school district computer. Previously, this student made a reference to the Columbine High School tragedy on social media. The student was immediately brought to the administrator's office and sat with the assistant principal and guidance counselor.

When I was brought into the conversation, I explained to the student, in the presence of the guidance counselor and administrator, that they were not in any trouble with me. Periodically throughout our conversation, I repeated the same and had the student repeat it back to me to ensure they understood. When we discovered the student had purchased knives on a website and they had recently been delivered, I explained my concern and made a request of the student.

I said, "Hey, buddy, do me a favor. Let me just make sure you don't have any knives or weapons on you."

Before I started, I told the student everything that was going to happen. I checked the student's backpack, pockets, shoes, and locker to make sure there weren't any weapons present, which there weren't. I also had the assistant principal and guidance counselor sitting there with me so other people were present. This also took place in the administrator's office, so it was not done in some cold, dark, scary room at the police station.

I'm never strip-searching a child, nor am I hovering with a spotlight over them. On TV, we see those theatrical interrogations in a dark, scary room with the officer asking, "Where were you at 2:40 yesterday afternoon?"

Instead, my interrogations are done with respect. Children deserve respect the same as adults. I talk to people like I would want to be spoken to; like I would want someone to treat my kids if I weren't around. Sometimes these conversations and interventions have to happen because students make impulsive statements on social media. Sometimes they bring things that would be considered contraband into school because they want to be cool or because they're not thinking about the consequences of their actions or how someone might perceive what they bring in. In those cases, I have to search school bags and lockers because it's my job to keep my schools safe.

Chapter 3: Humanizing Policing

When you get to work with students, you have the ability to positively impact their lives with every interaction you have. Every time you engage with them, you can let them know they are seen and they are important. When you know them by name, they know you see them for who they really are. There is so much power in greeting kids by their names and asking about something meaningful to them. To a kid who may feel invisible, this lets them know they are seen.

With as much power as we have to positively impact a child's life, we also have the potential ability to negatively impact a child's life. As police officers in a school building, we can be seen as very imposing figures to them. We have to be mindful of how we carry ourselves and how we communicate with kids through our tone, body language, and stance. If we aren't aware of how we are being perceived, we run the risk of creating a barrier between ourselves and our students. We risk potentially traumatizing students who have gone through adverse childhood experiences (ACEs), have had negative interactions with the police, or have negative stereotypes or perceptions towards police officers.

As an SRO, one of our jobs is to bridge the gap between cops and kids. By humanizing ourselves, we can build positive relationships with students and instill a positive perception of the role of police officers. I like to use three techniques to accomplish this: consistency, honesty, and patience.

I want the students to be familiar with me, so I have all of my kids from elementary school to high school call me Officer Beth. That being said, parents still get to decide how their children interact with and address other adults. Depending on culture and upbringing, some parents prefer their children to address adults by their title and last name, like Mrs. Sanborn, and I would never argue with a parent about that. However, I do allow my kids to use my first name with the appropriate title of Officer. Depending on the circumstances, people call me Officer Beth, Officer Sanborn, Detective Sanborn, Dr. Sanborn, Mrs. Sanborn, or Greg and Katie's mom. I don't get hung up on the name they call me, as long as it's said with respect.

I had a student who regularly walked by my office and one day yelled out "Beeeeettttttth!" as a greeting. I didn't see that as appropriate, so I needed to address it. Rather than embarrassing him in front of his friends and creating a barrier in communication, I simply pulled him aside and told him, "I'm not your friend. I will treat you with respect, but you have to do the same for me. I will allow you to call me Beth, but please include 'Officer' in front of it so it's not so disrespectful." When you address these situations using the proper tone and language rather than turning it into disciplinary action, it opens the conversation by creating a learning opportunity.

Once you establish familiarity and consistency, you can build relationships with students through vulnerability. In policing, you'll often find officers who are very guarded with personal information and won't give you any details regarding their family, spouse, kids, or where they live. Though I don't recommend sharing your home address with students, I do recommend sharing information about who you are as a person. Doing this will remind them you are a human, just like them.

I tell all my students about my biological children. My students know their names and what they look like because I have their pictures in my office. I tell them how my son graduated from North Penn High School and is going to Gwynedd Mercy University, and how my daughter is in 10th grade at North Penn High School. I share that my daughter is in the school play, and my son plays *Dungeons and Dragons* and *Magic: The Gathering*. We talk about my family vacations to the Pocono Mountains. They know my husband used to be a police officer before he retired, and I tell the kids I love dogs, but my own dog drives me crazy!

The Missing Piece

In being vulnerable, I can find commonalities between myself and my students. Conversations around food are usually the way to go. Everyone loves food, so I'll share my favorite restaurant with students. If I find out one of my students works at the local Mexican restaurant, I'll ask how good the guacamole is or if they recommend the enchiladas. I like to have these discussions with students because it creates a bond that can be used as a foundation for a relationship.

Finding these common denominators helps to humanize me. I don't want them to think I'm some robot walking around the hallways without any thoughts, feelings, or opinions. I want them to know I'm a mom, and when I get out of work, I take off this uniform and throw on my yoga pants, hoodie, and a pair of Nikes. That's who I am and when I feel most comfortable. This also makes students more comfortable talking with me, which, in turn, encourages them to use their voices. I want students to know their opinions matter to me. Not only can I see them, but I can hear them, and I value their thoughts and preferences. I love asking my students for their advice. I may ask them what the latest TikTok trends are or what kind of new sneakers I should get. Even if I don't always take their advice, I will still ask for it. I want them to feel like they have input and have the power of making decisions. If I notice one of my students always has her nails painted, I may ask her what color nail polish I should get at my next manicure appointment.

When people see the police uniform, they generally have an automatic response. Though a lot of different emotions come up for people, they usually have a heightened sense of curiosity, wonder, or concern, depending on their own personal experiences or preconceived notions about police officers. I realize my uniform could make people uncomfortable, so it's something I always have at the front of my mind. When I see my own mother and I'm in uniform, her demeanor towards me changes. She acts a little differently, and she gets a little fidgety because of the feeling the uniform elicits. If my own mother acts differently around me, then I know I need to be extra aware when

49

it comes to my students and their families. Though it doesn't mean I should avoid wearing a uniform, it does mean I need to be consciously aware that the uniform may elicit different feelings for different people.

Depending on the age group, I try to use my uniform to my advantage. In elementary schools, kids think it's super cool. They can't even make eye contact with me because they're so busy staring at my duty belt and asking questions about it. "Is that a gun? Is that your taser?" They're still learning boundaries, so they sometimes try to touch the tools on my belt. In those cases, I have to say, "Thank you, guys. These are my tools, and we can talk about all of my tools, but please don't touch them. Let's remember to keep our hands to ourselves."

At that age, they have received lessons on how the police are community helpers who come to save us if we have any problems or if we're concerned, scared, or hurt. They trust me because they weren't taught anything to the contrary. I like to stand up in front of the classroom and ask them if they can guess what I do for a living.

They shout out, "Cop!" or "You're the police!" Then, I tell them I'm a fireman. When they say, "No, you're not a fireman," I ask, "Well, how do you know I'm a police officer?"

Then, that starts the conversation. I ask, "What am I wearing that lets you know I'm a policeman?" They yell out the different items they see on me, like my badge, gun, taser, handcuffs, walkie-talkie, and even my keys. They are always fascinated by my toolbelt, and I like to talk about my tools with them, so it removes the fear and the unknown surrounding it.

Believe it or not, some elementary students have the forethought to say, "You have a gun. You can't have a gun in school."

I'm always very impressed by this, so I tell them I love the way they're thinking because it's a very complex thought. Then, I explain to them why it's okay for me to carry a gun by asking about different tools in relation to a profession.

I ask them, "Are you allowed to bring a knife to school?"

The class responds in unison, "NOOOOO!"

"But what if you're the cook in the cafeteria, would you have a knife?"

Then, they say "YESSSSS."

"Are you allowed to bring a box cutter to school?"

Again, they respond, "NOOOOO!"

"But what if you're the custodian and you need to open a package of paper?"

Then they answer, "YESSSSS."

I tell them it's one of the tools that help me do my job and keep them safe. I use their curiosity to my advantage, as an opportunity to educate them and let them know they don't have to be afraid of me.

Middle schoolers are a bit trickier because they're going through adolescence and are divided between two camps: the too-cool-for-school kids and the ones who are more like my elementary school kids. The too-cool-for-school kids might walk past me in the hallway, throw a shoulder at me, and say, "What, cop?" It's not personal. They're trying to figure out who they are, what kind of person they want to be, and where they belong, so they usually think it's fun to show off in front of their friends because that's part of what kids do as they grow up. My response to that is to make eye contact (because they love to look back at me and wait for a response) and give that one-raised-eyebrow "mom look" with pursed lips and tilted head to ask, "You ok? Do you need me? Everything all right?"

The ones who are more like my elementary school kids come up with more advanced questions like, "Did you ever shoot anyone?" or "Have you arrested anyone" or "Can I see your taser?" Those are the kids whom I can be goofy with and get away with walking through the cafeteria pretending to talk on my banana phone. They come up to me and I'll talk into the banana and say, "Hold on a second, I gotta talk to this kid," then put the banana down.

While I can goof off with middle schoolers somewhat, I still have to be incredibly cautious with my interactions. I will answer their questions, but in a way to focus on the positive and put their minds at ease that I am there to protect and to keep everyone safe. I want them to know I am there to prevent a problem from ever happening. Then, I have to tell them, "NO, I will not let anyone see my taser. It's a tool, not a toy, remember?" and "NO, I won't handcuff you either." Then, I remind them I love my job entirely too much to lose it by crossing any boundaries that might be considered inappropriate.

I started as an SRO in January 2015, which was midway through the school year. The school year was already in flow, and students had their groove. I remember being scared to death when I walked into the high school building. All of my personal feelings of self-consciousness and insecurity, that I had when I was in high school, came flooding back.

Our high school is not easy to navigate, and the stairways go in every direction. When I was walking the hallway on one of my first days, I was just about to walk past two girls wearing Ugg boots, black yoga pants, and hoodie sweatshirts, each with a Starbucks drink in their hands. They looked at me, put their hands in the air, and said "Hands up. Don't shoot," which originated after the police-involved shooting of Michael Brown on August 9, 2014, in Ferguson, Missouri. At that moment, I had a choice to make. It could have instantly turned into an adversarial situation, so I made a split-second decision. I put my hand on my chest and said, "Oh dang, that hurts me. Girls, I'm new here, and I don't know where J Hall is. Can you help me?" They said yes, and we started walking together.

Disclaimer: I totally knew where J Hall was, but it was the farthest hallway I could think of to give us time to walk and talk. A "walk and talk" is a great tool to use with students who are uncomfortable with making eye contact because you can walk parallel to each other and still have a conversation. It also helps when students are stressed and need to burn off some excess energy. Either way, at that moment, I opted to use it as an opportunity to walk with these girls for a few minutes and just have a nonsensical chat.

After that, there were a lot of times I walked the high school hallways and students asked, "Are you a narc?"

I just told them, "Nope, I'm a real-deal police officer."

I wasn't going to yell at them or assert my dominance over them because I was trying to build a relationship with them. Remember, they never had a police officer regularly appear in school before. They were trying to figure out why I was there and what they should expect out of me. They were figuring me out, just like I was figuring them out.

Even though I didn't have a ton of students in high school that year who were coming to me for support, I was still proud to go to graduation that first year. There was a collective excitement between students, families, and staff that was just intoxicating. It was incredible to be there and, for the first time, feel like a part of the celebration, instead of being an outsider, working the graduation ceremony as an uninvolved patrol officer. Fast forward a few years to the present, and I have an extraordinary number of students tell me I'm the coolest cop ever.

Chapter 4: Bridging the Gap

During my 25 years of police work, I've oftentimes noticed kids don't like cops and cops don't like kids. Now, that is an unfair, broad-sweeping overgeneralization, but let me explain. Often, interactions between kids and cops occur on a Friday or Saturday night at a large, underage drinking party. Impaired kids can be unpredictable, dangerous, and quite adversarial because a person's fight or flight response can take many forms. They may try to run and potentially get lost or hurt. They may try to jump in a car and drive away, risking a vehicle accident, serious bodily injury, damage, or death. They may stay and become "the most experienced attorney on the planet," because a drunken 16-year-old almost always says, "I know my rights," but they rarely ever do. Our other favorite is an impaired teenager who asks, "Do you know who my father is?" "Don't you have anything better to do?" or "Didn't you ever drink when you were a kid?" I'm sure you can imagine how well these interactions go over.

Other times, cops and kids interact when groups of kids get together and do things they might not ordinarily do when alone. They may smash a mailbox, egg a house, or steal from a convenience store. The majority of these interactions are typically single events, which don't allow for rapport building or creating a relationship. As an SRO, my interactions with kids are different.

I get to see them when there is nothing particular going on and when they are comfortable and not defensive. Under these circumstances, they can see and understand I am an advocate for them. I want to stand up for them and protect them because, in a totally appropriate way, I love them like my own children. I want them to know that no other police officer is going to care about them as much as I do because I know them for who they are, not just the "dumb stuff" they've done.

Dr. Beth J. Sanborn

When the high school students are in crisis or freaking out, they come to me. They'll sit in my office and talk to me about what's going on. They know they can come to my office to calm down or de-escalate with me. There's power in that because they don't see me as a threat or adversary who is out to lock them up. They see me as a trusted adult.

Getting to that point took time though. It took time to build the relationships through all these tiny positive interactions where I addressed students by their names and asked them questions about their day or the clothing they were wearing. I may even ask a silly question about our school's bell schedule, even though I already know the answer, just to spark a conversation like, "Is today a Day 4 or Day 5 schedule?"

As an SRO, I get to interact with people on the day-to-day when they're not in crisis. A lot of other police officers only work with people who are victimized, in which case, the person is likely having the worst day of their life. They're already feeling heightened emotions, and they're not in a mindset to want to build a relationship with the police officer on the scene. At that moment, they have a need, and the responding officer sets out to deliver that need. I get it; I understand. But in school, we have something I call emotional neutrality. A school is a place where everyone is on their home field and in their comfort zone. We all wake up in the morning, and we come to school whether we are cranky, tired, or have any number of feelings. This is the daily routine, and typically, no one feels defensive or in crisis. As much as kids don't like being in school, they're comfortable for the most part because it's their norm. On their home turf, I can interact with a student without them feeling defensive or being in crisis. We can talk, laugh, and joke around with one another in a safe environment.

Outside of my students, it's also important to bridge the gap with parents. Sometimes, I'll see a parent who is knowingly or unknowingly parked illegally, waiting to pick up their child. When I walk up to their car, they may assume or prepare for a negative interaction. When I introduce myself, they usually say they've heard a lot about me. Then, I simply smile and let them know this area is just for buses, and not for parent pickup, and I would hate to have a bunch of students crossing through and interfering with the buses. I let them know the rules and expectations and politely remind them to make sure they park in the parents' area tomorrow. My approach is always to de-escalate any potentially adversarial conversation immediately through the way I approach and use my body language. Police conversations don't have to be hostile or unfriendly. You can still get your message across by being friendly.

SROs are bridging the gap by showing that not all interactions with the police have to be negative. Even if they're doing something wrong, whether they know it or not, there's always a way to talk to people. Because of my role, I have the advantage that, even if I don't know the person I'm approaching, they're likely a parent or caregiver of one of my students in school, and I'm going to see them for the next 180 days and even over the course of multiple years.

There's that one story we've all heard about the awful cop who pulled you over on the highway, who was rude and demeaning. It gets told time and time again at every party and family function. I have to have 100 positive interactions with families to negate just one of those negative experiences. Even though it's likely my positive interactions will never be shared with anyone, it just might cause someone to think twice about sharing their negative encounter so freely. It is unfortunate we have to work twice as hard as others to overcome this negative stigma, but the benefits are well worth the effort, and I look at it as a welcome challenge.

That's why establishing credibility is so important. It helps me to be able to act as an informal counselor/mentor to students. When you meet someone for the first time, there's a good chance you might not 100% believe what they say or their perception may be skewed. For example, a passerby called the school recently because she drove past a vehicle in the school parking lot that had been vandalized. The car in question had male and female explicit genitalia drawn on it, in what appeared to be peanut butter. This passerby was horrified and accused the school of permitting bullying. When I located the driver of the vehicle, I learned it was not bullying, but a prank played on him by his friend group. He appreciated the concern but assured me he was fine and there was no cause for alarm.

When it comes to bullying, I often take phone calls from parents who report their child is getting bullied and that "no one is doing anything about it." In these instances, I rely heavily on the credibility I have established within my schools, and the parents and I discuss a few topics. First, I ask if the child has reported any of the bullying instances to anyone at school. It's incredibly difficult to intervene and prevent it if no one knows there is a problem or a concern. Second, I encourage the parent and child to refrain from engaging in the drama, whether it be in person or via social media. Bullying is one-way communication, but once the student replies in defense by going on their own attack, it then becomes a social conflict. At that point, we would have a discussion about conflict. We all experience conflict throughout our lives, and we must learn coping skills or ways to avoid it. Finally, I may ask if they are aware of the interactions their child has with the said bully at school. Sometimes, these incidents arise as a result of friends, who quickly become enemies, then revert back to being friends again.

When children complain to their parents (and don't we all enjoy a good complaining session), they rarely disclose their own participation. As a parent, you are trying to protect your child to the best of your ability, and you should! I completely understand that. But in the majority of these situations, I am often able to share the other side of the story, the parts parents aren't initially privy to.

I tell both students and their caregivers to think of me as the alley bumpers alongside a bowling lane. As long as a student's bowling ball keeps rolling forward towards those pins, that's progress. I am just the bumper, who sometimes has to guide them back on course when it looks like they're heading towards the gutter.

I don't want any of my kids to become gutter balls.

I don't just tell kids that. I truly mean it. I prove that to them by giving out my work cell phone number and showing them if they text me, I will actually respond to them. I show it by not getting them in trouble when they're eating in the hallways, sitting under the stairwell, hanging out in the bathroom too long, or taking a stroll around the school before they go back to class. When my actions reflect the words I tell them, they go home and tell their parents that Officer Beth is pretty cool.

When the school announced in a newsletter that there was now a police officer in the school, parents may have been concerned about this new unknown position in their child's school. But the students told their parents, "No, it's okay. It's just Officer Beth. She's the best." The students vouched for me, so their parents wanted to know more. I have invested time getting to meet parents at extracurricular events so they could put a face to my name, meet the police officer assigned to their child's school, and see the smile on my face. They see me interact with their kids, but even more important, they see how their kids interact with me. I made the effort, knowing some may have never had a prolonged encounter with a police officer unless they were in a car accident, had a medical emergency, or were a victim of a crime. It may have been the first positive interaction they had with an officer, so I smiled at them, let them know my ideology, and shared how I want to help their children.

Once the students vouched for me, the parents vouched for me too. Now, when I tell parents their kids are vaping in the bathrooms or there's THC usage, they're more likely to listen and ask questions. Parents know I'm not there to trap their children or criminalize their behavior. I legitimately want them to grow up to be healthy, safe, and productive adults.

Dr. Beth J. Sanborn

If parents don't like the services their children are getting, everybody is going to know about it. If they aren't happy there is a cop in their kid's school, they're going to demand they be removed. Fortunately, I was able to get my parents on my side.

We recently had an event at our elementary school called "Walk, Bike, or Roll to School Day" in celebration of Earth Day. As the SRO, I helped with the event to make it safe for all the students who participated. I was the last stop when the students got to school, and I told them they could head over to the pavilion and park their bikes.

To every student, I ended my welcome with "Have a great day at school!" I must have said it about 400 times.

The best part was that all of the students responded, "Thanks, Officer Beth," and their parents got to see that positive interaction between me and their child.

One of the parents actually came up to me and asked, "Are you Officer Beth?"

I smiled and said, "I am."

When she told me she was a school board member, I was a little nervous because a parent like that has power and could have me removed from the school. I gave her a giant smile and simply said it was nice to meet her, and she told me she heard the most wonderful things about me. This work is truly where my heart is, so hearing that meant a lot to me.

I treat all of these kids like they're my own. These small interactions are the most important because they bridge the gap for anyone who sees them. SROs are not just police officers stationed at schools; we are law enforcement officers who truly believe in fostering the success of children from a young age. Students, parents, school staff, and board members all need to know we aren't looking to "catch" your children. We want to teach them and support them in their growth to be amazing, productive members of society, just like you! When we do "catch" them, we want to catch them doing good.

Chapter 5: Not Your Traditional Precinct

Being a law enforcement officer in a school building is such a unique experience because SROs are given the opportunity to have positive interactions in a safe setting with students, parents, and school staff. In my role, I am fortunate enough to have been given an office by the school district. Not every SRO is given office space, but mine is located within the high school. It's just like any other teacher or administrator's office, but this one is all mine.

Even though it's the SRO's office, it's not set up like the usual mobile or remote police station. There isn't a check-in desk at the front with a sign-in sheet and someone patrolling it with a serious look on their face. There's no holding cell for students who are misbehaving. My office is not your traditional precinct, and I've been very intentional in creating this space. For starters, it is green everywhere. I have so many plants; it's like a greenhouse. There's a book called *The Green Cure*, which focuses on how calming it can be looking at greenery like plants, bushes, grass, trees, and leaves. That's how I ended up with the idea of transforming my office into a green space. It's softer, and the goal is for it to be therapeutic for anyone who might be in distress.

My plants always grow really well, despite the fact that my office has no windows or sunlight. After my first two years as an SRO, I gave some of them away at the end of the school year and took the rest back to the police station over summer break. As time went by, the plants grew massively, making transportation much more difficult. Luckily, the summer school crew offered to take care of them for me while I was away.

There is one plant in particular, that I bought during my first year as an SRO. I call it my SRO plant because it has lasted the longest and has grown to the point where it almost wraps itself around my office. I will never give that one away. I take care of it the most because it represents me and my career.

I also have fidget toys, essential oils, crystals, candy, and food. If you haven't noticed yet, candy has also played a role in establishing myself at the school. If you want students to feel comfortable coming to your office, keep it stocked with candy – not the cheap stuff either. I buy the good stuff, and I also take requests. Fun-size Hershey's, Reese's, Nestles, Sour Patch, Gummy Bears, Blow Pops, Swedish Fish, Twix, Twizzlers, Snickers, Heath, and even Lemonheads and Warheads – if you request it, I'll stock it!

My office isn't a 24/7 trick-or-treat experience though. I have a rule. Students can come to my office once a day and take one piece of candy, BUT they have to engage in conversation with me. They must greet me and ask at least one basic question like, "How is your day going?" or tell me something going on in their lives. I've found this to be a great way to start relationships with students and continue to build them with every interaction after that.

Word spread recently that the snacks were restocked in my office. A student ran up to me and asked, "You got any snacks?"

I heard exactly what she said, but I said, "I'm sorry?" She said it again, and I responded, "I'm sorry. Did you say 'Good morning, Officer Beth. How are you?'" When she repeated what I said, I replied, "I'm great. How are you? I don't know if we've ever spoken before. What's your name?"

After she told me, we walked to my office, and I told her where the snacks were. She grabbed something, and I told her, "My rule is, you can come in once a day to grab a snack, but you have to talk to me." The next day when I saw her, I greeted her by name. When she came to my office, she said, "You got any snacks?" I folded my arms and looked at her without saying anything. Then she said, "Hey, Officer Beth."

Then I smiled and said, "Yes, I got some snacks. You know where they are." I laughed, and we engaged in some very brief chit-chat before she went on her way.

I have spent a good amount of money, out of my own pocket, because there is no way I want anyone to mistake my office for a disciplinarian's room. I wanted it to look different from their classrooms and even the principal's office. It's calming and soothing, and a good place to go to be distracted for a few minutes.

One of my new favorite additions is a stuffed teddy bear. It's like any other stuffed animal, but it's made with alpaca fur, which is incredibly fluffy and plush. The first time I bought an alpaca fur stuffed animal was while I was on vacation with my daughter. That evening, I was sitting on the couch and realized how surprisingly calming it was to pet. It was like petting a real dog. There's enough research on how petting animals can reduce blood pressure because you tend to take deeper breaths and inhale more oxygen. It's such a great tool for calming nerves so I decided to bring it into school. I found my students always picking it up when they stopped by my office, and some would stop by in the morning just to hold it before starting their day. Since my students loved it, I decided it deserved a permanent home on one of the chairs used by my visitors. I wound up buying another one just for my daughter.

My students always ask me where I get such cool stuff. To be honest, I spend a lot of time and money looking for great tools to add to my office. I buy a lot of fidget toys because they come in handy. Students tend to share things they might otherwise find uncomfortable or difficult to navigate when they're in a welcoming environment. When you do have to talk about sensitive topics, like sexual assault or making any type of personal disclosure, it's easier to have those conversations in a softer space. If you're talking about something sensitive or are feeling particularly vulnerable, it helps to be sitting in a comfortable chair and having something to occupy your hands, like a fidget, so you don't necessarily have to make eye contact.

Eye contact can be very intimidating for many students, which makes them less likely to talk. Our natural reaction when we feel discomfort or shame is to lower our heads and look at the ground, avoiding eye contact. You may have noticed your teenager reaching for their cell phone during difficult conversations, and it's not because they're ignoring you or being rude, but because they feel uncomfortable. When students can occupy their hands with a fidget or stuffed animal, they feel less pressure to make eye contact and are significantly more likely to open up.

I try to create a relaxing sensory space. One thing I haven't researched thoroughly yet is playing music as a therapeutic measure in lowering heart rates. Right now, I play pop music because I like it and most of my students do too. Some people say my office reminds them of a spa, but I don't want to go overboard with spa music. I truly love my office. It's my comfort zone, and I want it to be my students' comfort zone in the building too, so they know they have a place to go when they need it.

If a student calls their parent or caregiver from my office, many times they'll say, "I'm in the cop's office."

I laugh a little and ask, "May I have your phone, please?" Then I get on the phone and say, "Hi, it's Officer Beth. Your child is not here because they are in trouble. Your kid is a little upset right now, and I offered them a spot to calm down so they wouldn't be the center of attention and the subject of someone's dramatic social media post." That explanation has always been well-received and appreciated by caregivers, especially if they haven't seen my office before.

Over the course of seven years working in the school district, parents have come to know me. They know there's a difference between being in "the cop's office" and sitting with Officer Beth. When kids come to my office, they know it's a place to have a bottle of water, grab a piece of candy, take a couple of deep breaths, and play with some of the best fidget toys in the building.

I've put in a lot of work to create a space that is sensory-friendly because when anyone is in distress, the presence of law enforcement can heighten that stress. But I want people to know not all law enforcement interactions need to be stressful. I want people to see me as a community helper, like we teach our elementary school children, because that's my job and I'm passionate about helping my community.

Dr. Beth J. Sanborn

My SRO Plants

A Typical Day at the Office

The Missing Piece

One of My Favorite Lessons

Part II: Informal Counselor/Mentor

One of my favorite parts about what I do, and quite possibly the most important, is serving as an informal counselor and mentor. While my training allows me to be serious and formal, I also love helping people, which is the reason I became a police officer to begin with. Students don't always need a cop or another rule enforcer. Sometimes, they need to feel seen and heard by an adult to whom they feel comfortable talking. Going to an "authority" figure can sometimes come with a stigma and cause them to avoid having a conversation about what is bothering them or going on in the building. Even though I am wearing a uniform, my kids know I do not work *for* the school, and they can speak to me casually and comfortably. That type of relationship doesn't form overnight, and I don't take it lightly. I work really hard to build and maintain relationships in my school community, especially when it comes to my students. Though the techniques I've learned over the years weren't part of my formal training, all of them have helped me build the rapport I have today as an informal counselor/mentor in the school district.

Chapter 6: Building Trust

When I work toward building trust, I focus on being genuine and straightforward. That means explaining what I am doing and why I am doing it, so I don't appear to be subjective. This is especially important when working with kids because I don't want them to feel as though I'm picking on them.

If I am brought into a conversation with a guidance counselor, parent, or administrator, emotions are more than likely higher than usual. It's reasonable to assume they are most likely agitated as a result of a conflict of some sort. In those situations, my first response is to encourage empathy. I may ask them to look at the situation from the perspective of the other person and ask why they're feeling the way they are. That's not always what people expect to hear from a cop, but they know me and know I'm being genuine with them. I use the strategy of lowering my voice, speaking a bit more slowly, and leaning forward while I converse. Lowering my voice and slowing down my speech tends to calm people and force them to concentrate on what I'm saying.

One of the common conflicts I have to mediate is between a student who doesn't want to go to school and their parents. The parent is usually fed up, doesn't know how to get their child to school, and wants to set all these ground rules, but the student doesn't like the rules they have at home. The way I usually lead that conversation is by opening the dialogue like this:

"Listen, you're a kid. I don't mean any disrespect by that, but you're under 18 years old, so in the eyes of the law, you're seen as a child. Again, no disrespect, but that's just the reality of your age."

Then, I wait for them to acknowledge that. It could be as simple as a "yeah" or a head nod. From there, I might say,

"So, here's the problem. Since you're a kid, your parents are responsible for you until you turn 18, which means they get a say in what you do and what you can't do. They get to set the house rules. You might not agree with them, and you might not like them, but unfortunately, that's the reality of it. The dangerous part of this is there's no magical door that opens up the day you turn 18. You don't wake up with all the money, means, and resources that allow you to suddenly get a job and move out into your own place. You may gain a little more independence in the eyes of the law and be able to make some decisions on your own, but once you turn 18, there are certain things you lose, like all the legal protections put in place for kids."

When I explain what turning 18 really looks like, it gets rid of the fear of the unknown. It also sheds light on the magical world students think opens up to them when they turn 18. Once they realize waking up on their 18th birthday will still look a lot like when they woke up at 17, it makes them think. When I build trust, I focus on removing the surprise factor from situations by explaining every bit of the process. That type of communication also takes time through either one long conversation or a series of short conversations over a period of time. Anything I say, I make sure my actions back it up. If I tell a student I'm going to be here for them, I'll check in with them, ask how they're doing, and address them by name. I'm going to make sure I do that because if I don't, I risk losing their trust.

In my high school, there are about 1,400 students and only one of me, but when I say I'm going to address students by name, I try my best. Especially at the beginning of the year, I may get students' names wrong, but I tell them ahead of time to please be patient with me. There's no disrespect intended, and I am doing my best. Letting them know this ahead of time also helps to build trust. Then, students like to challenge me by randomly popping in and yelling, "What's my name?"

Another way I build trust is by giving all the students my work cell phone number, which was issued by the school district. Although

The Missing Piece

this isn't something every SRO needs to do or is required to do, it's a big leap of faith for me. It's plastered on my office door, and I will write it on the whiteboard when I go into classrooms. I want staff and students to know that if they're ever scared or worried, if something is bothering them, or if they've got that pit in their stomach and need someone to talk to, I'm available. When they feel alone and don't have anyone to reach out to, they can reach out to me. If they need someone at three o'clock in the morning because they're freaked out and worried, they know they can call me or text me. I'm going to wake up. I may answer the phone all confused, but I will answer.

In all the years I've been doing this, nobody has ever prank-called me. When I give my number out at school assemblies at the start of the year, my phone blows up for the next 10 to 15 minutes because students are trying to verify if I gave them my real number. Once that's out of their system, students know not to take advantage of it. I tell them I'm willing to give them my number because I trust them, and no other cop I've met is going to do that.

Surprisingly, I've had a lot of students reach out to me for support. I've had 4 A.M. text messages come through from students who were in crisis. Once I feel like they have moved beyond that critical moment, I will ask them if we can revisit this conversation in daylight hours because I'm old and need sleep. Sometimes they apologize, but I tell them there's no need because I am here for them and want them to feel better. The important thing then is that I do follow up with them the next day and check in to see how they're feeling. That follow-up is the icing on the cake of trust.

Typically, if I get an isolated text message, it's usually one student who is in crisis or who has a question. But sometimes, I get a whole series of texts that come through simultaneously, which usually means someone posted some type of threat or something concerning on social media, and a ton of students have seen it. In those cases, some students take screenshots, send them to me, and tell me they're scared.

Dr. Beth J. Sanborn

I have an obnoxious notification tone with a piercing ding noise, so it forces me to wake up if messages come through at night. I also keep the LED flash on for notifications so if, for some reason, I don't wake up to the noise, the visual flash of light surely will.

I remember a student who came to me, particularly despondent-looking one day. I knew her by name and interacted with her regularly. She knew she could come to my office if she was ever struggling. One day, she came to my office and stood in the doorway. She had that look – brow furrowed, head down, and shoulders slumped. When I asked what was wrong, she told me she had a really strong urge to cut. I responded by inviting her to sit down. I talked slower and a little quieter, trying to de-escalate her. I asked what she usually did to calm herself down when she found herself facing a crisis, and she said she listens to music.

"What kind of music?" I asked.

"Country music," she replied.

"New country or old-school, bluegrass country music?"

"New country," she said.

So, I pulled out my phone and put on my favorite Kane Brown song. I started singing and dancing along and about 30 seconds in, I could see her body language change. She smiled a little, her brow unfurrowed, her shoulders relaxed back, and her head and chin were both up. I knew it was helping her at the moment. Then she smiled and asked, "Can I get a piece of candy?"

"Of course! How are you feeling?" I asked.

She said, "I'm okay.

"Are you okay to go back to class?'"

She said, "Yes."

The Missing Piece

After having a student come to me with the urge to cut, I knew there was a chance this student could be actively suicidal. I wasn't just going to send her back to class being the only person who knew about this. This was an important piece of the puzzle. Just because I was able to de-escalate the situation in the moment, it didn't guarantee I would be there next time or that she wouldn't run to the bathroom after she left my office. So, I asked, "Can I call mom and email your guidance counselor and principal to let them know we just talked?"

She agreed because that wasn't my first time interacting with her. All of these crises are part of the puzzle, and we have to help put everything back together. So, when I called mom and informed guidance and the administration, I didn't know the immediate end result. I don't know if her guidance counselor called her down or if her mom came to pick her up from school. What I do know is when she walked out of my office, she was smiling with her candy in hand, and she felt better at that moment, which was a dramatic shift from the first time I saw her. The important takeaway here is that I'm just one person on her support team. I don't have the long-term solutions to her problems, but at the moment, I was the bandage she needed, and she trusted me enough to come and be vulnerable. I let the rest of her team know so we could all offer continuing support to her.

Another student came to me because she was very upset when she discovered her boyfriend had a Dropbox account with all of these pictures of naked breasts from different girls. Since the assumption was that they were pictures of peers, and potentially in high school and underage, this was legally considered child pornography. When I found out her boyfriend went to a different school in another jurisdiction, I wrote up a police report and handed it off to the other department for investigation. This initial interaction helped me to develop a good rapport with her. When she first walked into my office, she sat in my chair with her knees pressed into her chest and was rocking back and forth because she was so upset. During our conversation about what she found on her boyfriend's phone, I learned she was interested in

Cherokee folklore. She told me the story about the White Wolf, which represents purity, and the Black Wolf, which represents chaos. She explained you can't have one without the other, and that idea resonated with her.

Years later, just before she graduated, I gave her a keychain with the black and white wolves. She must have told her parents about it because her dad came up to me in the midst of graduation with thousands of people on the field. He asked if I was Officer Beth and told me who his daughter is. He wanted me to know the impact I had on his daughter was really meaningful and that she talked about me a lot. Even in moments of crisis for students, positive experiences can come out of them.

Chapter 7: Long-Term Relationship Building

I've been doing this job long enough to be fortunate to interact with families across multiple generations. Back in the day, I remember responding to calls for families with young children. Fast forward, now those kids are parents, and I'm interacting with their kids. I have built long-standing, generational relationships with the people I'm serving.

My first actual arrest was following a domestic disturbance call where I ended up arresting the male as a result of a physical dispute between the couple. As the case progressed, I established a working relationship with the female victim. Even after the case was all said and done, she continued to live in the township, so our paths crossed quite regularly. She also had children, so I interacted with them when I was on police calls in their geographic vicinity all during their childhood. Over the years, they sometimes needed police services and required our intervention, but it never became an adversarial situation. Our main goal was to de-escalate the situation by separating people, kicking someone out for the night, or just making them go their separate ways to cool off.

During those 911 calls, I interacted with the daughter, who was a baby when I previously arrested the male figurehead in the house, and I had the opportunity to see her grow up. Now, she's a mom. When we show up at her house or in the neighborhood, she brings her children out and introduces us. We have come to know her kids' names and hang out with them. I remember one of her kids sitting on the front porch, wearing a diaper and a tiny white t-shirt, eating a little bag of Doritos. Her children are growing up and have entered the school system, so I interact with them regularly and greet them with a smile. I have a relationship with grandma, mom, and grandchildren now, which I think is really special.

Despite the fact that she and her family have had numerous interactions with law enforcement over the course of many years, there are no negative associations with our police department. Because we treat people well and with dignity and respect, we are able to build those long-term relationships with the people in our community. Just because someone commits a criminal act doesn't mean they need to be disrespected or treated poorly. It doesn't make them a bad person; it just makes them a person who made a poor decision. In fact, this family regularly addresses us by our first names – that's how well they know us.

Building these long-standing relationships makes our job easier because we don't have to be concerned about how the public is going to react during our interactions. They know us, and we know them, so everyone knows what to expect from one another.

There's a family in the community who was going through a divorce and had repeated domestic disputes that required our intervention. They were separated, but their daughter was still in school, so they remained within the geographic region of the district. Now, the daughter is a mom, and her child goes to the elementary school in our district. I remember when she was pregnant, and now I get to see her son all the time.

This is another situation where the mom and her son witnessed numerous interactions with the police while growing up, which could be potentially traumatizing for a lot of children when you really think about it. Imagine yourself as a little kid during a domestic dispute. Maybe you don't even have to imagine because you've experienced it. You are likely scared by the fight happening in your home between the people you love. Then, a police officer shows up. What is a child left to think other than worrying their parent or grandparent is going to get arrested and taken away? Experiences like that can truly impact a child through negative associations or even by triggering a trauma response.

The Missing Piece

Many people don't encounter the police at all throughout their life for anything other than being pulled over for a traffic violation or other innocuous passings at a convenience store. Despite the fact that the mother and her son just described had frequent interactions with law enforcement, they now have positive associations with the police. We smile at each other, I know his name and how to pronounce it correctly, and he gets so excited when he shows me his work at school. These small gestures let children know they are important and who they are matters. They encourage children to build a strong sense of identity and belonging in the community. Hopefully, as he gets older, he will take all of these positive experiences with him and tell people about the cool cop at his school, the one who sat at the lunch table with him and joined in during gym classes. I want to create enough positive interactions to overshadow any negative associations he may feel around the police. If I can make a big enough impact, he will remember the smiles and positivity at school instead of the officers responding to the disturbances at home.

When I think about building long-term relationships with my students, one middle school student, in particular, stands out. She was on probation for a case I was not involved with, so her probation officer regularly checked in with me and wanted to know if there had been issues with her at school. During middle school, she was always on the periphery of problems. Anytime there was drama, her name always came up with an asterisk next to it. She may not have been directly involved, but she was usually there, or it involved her friend group. Now, she's getting ready to graduate high school, and her name has not popped up on my radar in a few years. She got a full scholarship to the local college for a program she's interested in, and it just so happens to be the same college my son goes to. Naturally, I told her about him. Not only is it a way to humanize the badge and bridge the gap, but it's a way to show her we will still have a connection even after she graduates. When I saw her family member come to pick her up recently, I said, "I'm so proud of her. She's come such a long way. I was just talking to her about her bright future ahead." I wasn't just saying that to him; I truly meant it because her success is important to me.

When I work with families across generations, the relationship goes both ways. Just as much as I know about them, they know about me. Families know my husband's name, and some of them have met my kids. Although you may not see that in a big city police department, that's one of the perks of working in a smaller township. People know us by name, so it lessens the fear when we show up because we are a familiar face and they know what to expect. They understand we still have a job to do as law enforcement, but they know we are only responding to their behaviors and their reactions to those behaviors.

Officers who establish themselves as reasonable and are able to have a conversation without flying off the handle are more likely to build long-term relationships with their community members. If you're a resident in a particular area for an extended period of time and your police officers have also been around a long time, there's a good chance you're going to cross paths with them on more than one occasion. It might be on a 911 call, at the grocery store, or at school. We have the benefit of that small-town feel. As a police officer and an SRO, it's important to know my neighborhood and the people who live here. It's about being an invested stakeholder within the community, in addition to being a police officer for that same community.

When you think about the public outcry surrounding policing, the special action groups who want to reimagine police, and those who want a complete overhaul of law enforcement, what is it that they want from police officers? They are demanding police officers be better listeners and approach their job with a clearer mind. They want the police to be empathetic, to be respectful, to understand mental illness, and to recognize the needs of the community. Everything these groups want is at the core of the basic SRO training curriculum created by the National Association of School Resource Officers (NASRO). SROs learn how to act and how to interact with people. We look beyond the mere behavior and learn the "why" behind the behavior. We are more inclined to think and respond, instead of merely reacting.

Honestly, these practices are so ingrained in me that I sometimes forget when I'm not in my school environment. I might be at the grocery store smiling at everyone, and some people may recognize me as Officer Beth, and others who don't look at me with the expression of, "Are you one of *those* cops?" I've learned to be gregarious and outgoing. I'm the one who holds the door for people and offers to buy a kid a candy bar at the store. Of course, I always ask their parents first and then remind the child to eat their vegetables and wear their seatbelts.

This is my community, and I'm part of it. Despite what people see on the news, I know who I am as a police officer, and I know I create more good than I do harm. The media only shows the outliers on the news, the incidents that are newsworthy. They're not going to release breaking news about Officer Beth buying a candy bar for a kid at the convenience store, but those interactions happen more often than not. I don't do it for a social media post. I rarely snap a picture with a student. My only goal is to leave a family with a positive story and hope their experience with the friendly police officer results in a story that travels far and wide.

Sometimes, I like to go to extracurricular events when I'm off-duty and in personal clothes to cheer kids on. I go to the school plays with my kids because we love theater. I show up at art shows and school dances. In our district, we host Mini-THON, which is a charity dance marathon where students raise money to fight childhood cancer. I love to show up to Mini-THON in uniform. It's silly and self-deprecating to dance wearing my vest and duty belt with my keys clanking around, but the students enjoy it, and it makes me part of their community that way.

Because the kids in my area know me, they aren't afraid when they see me outside of school. There are more of them than there are of me, so they can pick me out easier than I can pick them out. If they're wearing a school shirt, then I more than likely know them and will interact with them. If I'm not sure, I can usually gauge their facial expression. Some kids get a little excited and I can see they recognize me, so I'll know it's safe to approach them. Some kids look at me and look right past me, which tells me I shouldn't interact at all. It is funny when I'm out at Target in a sundress and flip-flops and hear, "Hi, Officer Beth!" I get a big smile on my face and introduce my kids, if I'm with them, to "my other kids."

I was at Wawa recently, and four boys walked in. One of them said to another, "Isn't that your security guard?"

I was in uniform, laughed, and said, "Security guard? I'm a cop."

The boy said he meant security from the school because he sees me at school.

I told him, "Yep, that's me, but I'm a cop – for real!"

When I saw him the next day, I asked him what kind of ice cream he got because I saw him by the ice cream cooler before I left. He said he got a milkshake instead, but I used that as an opportunity to continue that relationship with him and interact with him in a positive way.

It's not just my students who recognize me; their parents do too. In fact, one summer, I was on vacation walking down Broadway in Saratoga, NY and heard "Officer Beth!" as a mom ran up to me to say hello. I was six hours from home, walking down the street, carrying a stuffed animal, and I was recognized! These moments reassure me that I'm doing my part in being more than just a police officer – I'm building long-term relationships with my community.

Chapter 8: Vulnerability

There are times when I have to cash in on the minor infractions I overlook for my students. It's like a barter system in my mind. If kids are roughhousing and I ask them to knock it off, I expect them to say, "Yes, Officer Beth. Sorry, Officer Beth," and comply. For the most part, it works.

Recently, I had two students who were slap-boxing each other, and it was clearly just two friends being silly and smacking each other around. I knew they were friends, and no one was getting hurt, but I was a little worried about one of them accidentally getting hit too hard and getting injured or the potential of it turning into an actual brawl. I also couldn't have other students see the slap-boxing and think I was going to tolerate it. It had the potential of sending the wrong message by letting students think they could play-fight too. I just walked up to them and said, "Hey, guys, please, knock it off. I know you're just playing, but hands to yourselves."

They both looked me dead in the eyes and continued smacking each other while maintaining eye contact with me!

At that point, I moved a little closer to them since we were in the midst of all these students. I told them, "You're disrespecting me. I understand you're playing around, and you want to look cool in front of your friends, but don't make me look bad to everyone else."

There's a level of trust and vulnerability that goes into saying that, but it's something the students can relate to. They don't want to look bad in front of their friends, and I don't want to look bad in front of the other students or administration because it could jeopardize the safety of the school and my job. Once that happens, there is no guarantee the next SRO is going to be quite as accommodating as I am.

Dr. Beth J. Sanborn

I hold students to certain expectations because I know they know how to behave. Students often only see the world through their lens as a teenager, which gets shaped by their experiences and what's happening to them in that moment. Sometimes I have to share with them how I'm seeing the same situation, through the lens of a police officer who has been doing this for 25 years. Not many adults, especially ones in positions of authority, will take the time to share their point of view in the hopes of having a constructive conversation, and that goes a long way.

When I came back to work after having both of my knees replaced, I was in a position that required me to be vulnerable with my students. I let them know I had undergone major surgery and wasn't in the best physical shape. I was already a little battered, and having to get involved in breaking up any physical fights could cause me more serious injury. I asked them to think about me in those moments. They were also very aware that if I got hurt in a fight and taken out of the building, there would be some other cop coming in, who they might not have the same relationship with.

Was that selfish? Maybe. But I knew, deep down, that none of them wanted to see me get hurt. Sometimes I just needed to remind them I'm a 47-year-old mom who was just coming back from major surgery and wanted to be there to protect and support them.

Vulnerability is about letting the students know you're not perfect. You may have times when you're a little broken, and it's okay to have bumps in the road. I share those struggles with my students, especially when it comes to mental health. I share my experiences with depression, anxiety, and eating disorders, and how I didn't have a great friend group when I graduated high school because I had been ostracized. Even to this day, I don't know why my friend group turned their backs on me. Have I gotten past it? Yes. Is it something I still hold on to? Absolutely. But I recognize these experiences have shaped who I am to this day.

The Missing Piece

Being able to understand what my students are going through puts me in a better position to interact with teenagers. I know what it's like to feel uncomfortable in your skin, to have a knot in the pit of your stomach, and to have that heavy feeling in your throat when you're anxious. I can empathize with them. Having these experiences helps me connect specifically with female students who may be struggling with any of those feelings.

A few years ago, I had a student who told me she was eating lunch every day on the bathroom floor by herself. I remember saying, "Absolutely not. That's unacceptable. You are not permitted to sit on the bathroom floor and eat lunch by yourself. You can come to my office and have lunch with me." I wasn't telling her it was unacceptable because it was a school violation (although it was); it was unacceptable because I didn't want her to feel alone. She felt comfortable enough to share that with me, and I wanted to validate her by showing I value her and she should value herself as a person as well.

So, she started coming to my office, and we had lunch together. I began asking about her interests so I could guide her toward a few different groups and clubs. Joining a club is a great way to make friends because you already share a common interest. She told me she felt like she was too old to make friends. Although I told her that's never the case, I understood what she meant. I definitely feel like I'm too old to make friends at this point in my life, but every now and then, I go out, meet someone new, and have a good conversation. Although I may never talk to that person again, I explained how it's important to continue to try, and do it again and again to build confidence in yourself.

If a student comes to me upset because their girlfriend was texting them the night before saying she wanted to kill herself, I explain how that's a lot of pressure to take on. I don't want a student to assume unnecessary burdens from a peer. I would never want my own child to struggle and feel like a friend's life is in their hands. I try to remind them it's not their burden to assume. They are children, no disrespect intended, and they need to focus

Dr. Beth J. Sanborn

on their English project, college applications, and algebra test, not whether or not their friend is going to kill themselves. That is too heavy of a burden for any child to carry.

As adults, we can encourage them to bring these concerns to our attention. When they do, we can remind them they are a really good friend for being supportive in this way. We need to help them see that getting professionals involved is the best way to support their friends who are in crisis. That's what we do; we remove that burden from them.

Although I believe in being vulnerable with my students, there are a few boundaries I stick to. I would never put anything on a student they may then feel responsible for, ever. I draw a hard line there. I also don't share if I was ever engaged in any unsavory behavior when I was in high school because I don't want to normalize it. I can, however, empathize with them. I can compare their stories with other students' experiences, without giving any identifying details. I might remind a student they aren't the only one who ever got in trouble for cheating on a test. Students have cheated on tests before, but they still went on to be productive adults.

Despite the number of times my students have asked me how many people I've arrested, or if I've ever tasered anyone, none of them have ever asked me if I've ever used drugs. Because I am so open while talking with my students, I don't think they've ever considered asking. If anyone did decide to ask, I wouldn't lie, I would simply respond, "It's just never been my thing." I talk to my students about personal aspects of my life, where appropriate. I share stories about my kids, my daughter's sweet sixteen, or my son's annoyance with college paperwork. I'm open to talking with them about those things because I know they can relate to them. If students were to pry into areas I don't feel comfortable discussing, I may respectfully tell them it's not something I feel is appropriate to discuss, then try to redirect the conversation in a more productive direction.

The Missing Piece

Sometimes, I feel like I am more guarded with school staff than I am with my students. It's an interesting dynamic because I'm still an outsider in the school building. I never complain about the frustrations of working in a school because I don't want to be perceived as displeased with my job, my schools, my principal, or the staff. Although I'd love to have a work friend who I can freely commiserate with, I have to be careful. I make sure to always portray the image of positivity and teamwork. I want my students to succeed, and I want to be part of the team that helps guide them toward constant progress, like the bowling alley bumpers I mentioned earlier. I want everyone to be happy and healthy, and I want to be a part of making sure that happens. When I am vulnerable with school staff, it's usually like talking to any other adult. I talk about my husband, my kids, dream vacations, cars, and mundane doctor's appointments. We talk about people problems, not work problems.

Vulnerability with parents also looks different. Some of the parents I've known for years, and others know me simply because their children talk about me. One of the parents at school is someone I used to play tennis with. I recently told her I was having a difficult time with my daughter, and she could empathize with me. My daughter was going through a phase where she didn't want to talk with me, and I was hurt. There I was, in my police uniform, freely admitting I struggled with the best way to handle a situation with my own child. Fortunately, though, my daughter's phase ended rather quickly.

Although I may not be as vulnerable with a parent I don't know as well, most parents at school know I'm a mother. They understand they're not just talking to a police officer; they're talking to a mom too. A mom of teens, nonetheless. When one of their children is having an issue, I often envision my own kids in that situation. Although I may not tell them that, they understand how I can empathize with them and how I want their children to succeed.

Even though I'm always trying to help my students, I also realize I am not a doctor, and I make sure my students and their families understand that as well. I can't diagnose or treat whatever issue they may have going on in their life. I'm more of a bandage. I can work with them at the moment to identify what is going on and get them to a better position for the time being, but someone else needs to take care of the long-term healing. My students know I will be by their side every step of the way until they can get that help, and I will more than likely check in on them as they are healing because I genuinely want them healthy.

Chapter 9: Advocating for Students

At one of our elementary schools, there was a first grader who had a number of discipline referrals. Her go-to response was violence, even when she wasn't provoked. She would walk into her classroom, see a student typing on their laptop, and shut the laptop on the student's fingers. There were other times she poked students with pencils. These behaviors simply aren't appropriate, and as a result, she received several write-ups, forcing her to see the principal. Intervention was mandatory in this case, so the student's caregiver was contacted.

The student's school support team had tried a few different interventions, but nothing worked. During a meeting, the student's caregiver was asked if they were comfortable with their child spending some time with me, her SRO. I had already done this for a number of other students over the years and was happy to see if it could help in this situation. The caregiver was on board with the decision, so I set up weekly meetings with the student and became a part of her Positive Behavioral Interventions and Support (PBIS) plan. PBIS is an evidence-based educational framework designed to support positive outcomes for students and is often used when students are struggling or exhibiting challenging behaviors.

Initially, when I first met with her, we sat together and simply coexisted. In an attempt to get her more involved in our meetings, I planned fun activities for us to do together like coloring, building Legos, or making paper airplanes. And, of course, I always brought snacks. As soon as we started spending more time together, the principal told me there had been a massive improvement in her behavior. There were no more write-ups or disciplinary issues. To me, that was a clear indication I played an important role in implementing her PBIS plan, and it worked. Maybe it was the mini-Oreos and strawberry milk, but I like to think I played my part too. She needed one-on-one time with an adult who didn't view her as a "bad" kid, someone to listen and pay attention to her.

I made it clear to the principal and her caregiver that I would be a regular part of her week. I had no intention of canceling appointments if she had a bad week. Her time with me was not a reward for good behavior or punishment for lack thereof. Instead, I made it clear a bad week was an opportunity for us to talk about what happened that week. During the year, I learned more about her, and we had fun during the time we spent together and talked about the "why" behind her behaviors. We built a solid relationship with each other, so I decided to buy her a special gift at the end of the school year – a stuffed yellow cat, which was her favorite animal in her favorite color.

Every student needs someone to advocate for them whether they're going through a difficult phase in their life or just having a bad day. Recently, one of my students was about to take her driving test, and she was really nervous. She failed the first time, so she felt even more pressure to pass this time. A few days before her test, she told me she was ready to retake it on the upcoming Monday. She said she'd been practicing and documenting all the time she spent driving. I smiled and cheered her on with small, encouraging messages.

These phrases can mean more to a child than you realize:

- "You've got this!"
- "You're ready for this."
- "Take a deep breath."
- "Don't rush yourself."
- "Trust your gut."
- And, of course, "Make sure your seatbelt is on!"

Although it might seem silly, those encouraging words were part of what got her through the test. Afterward, she told me how important the encouragement was to her, and how she was so happy she passed!

Another way I enjoy supporting my students is during their class presentations and other public speaking events. Public speaking frightens so many of my students to the point I can see them become nervous just telling me about the upcoming presentation. Naturally, I offer to help. I ask them if it is okay for me to show up for their presentation and stand or sit in the back of the classroom so they can make eye contact with me while presenting. Having me around during presentations has really helped ease their nerves because they can pretend they're having a conversation with me, with someone they're comfortable with, instead of looking at all their peers staring back at them.

Neither counseling nor mentoring have a defined set of expectations, and different people will have different needs from you at different times. Understanding that is one of the key aspects of being a good mentor. Kindness, generosity, and loyalty are all values good mentors should have, and I model that for my students.

When it comes to loyalty, I tell students they can be loyal friends without committing a criminal offense for that friend. If their friend gets into a fight, it doesn't mean they have to jump into the fight and start throwing punches. They can be loyal to friends without crossing boundaries. Oftentimes, when I speak with students after they've been involved in a fight, I learn they got involved only because their friend was fighting. So, I redirect the conversation by asking, "Wouldn't you have been a better friend if you prevented your friend from getting into the fight in the first place?" If students encourage each other to walk away, be the bigger person, and avoid drama, then neither gets in trouble, and no one risks getting hurt.

Student success is paramount. I advocate for that across the board. The administration, principal, assistant principal, and all school staff know me as being the kid cheerleader. I always want to give students space to explore their own identities and develop a sense of belonging in their community. When I'm presented with issues involving students, I identify what direction to take when addressing those issues with their success in mind. Sometimes I have to take a law enforcement approach and issue a citation, but that's not my first method of intervention. A citation typically results under a few specific circumstances, such as if a student causes harm to another and the victim's family is insistent upon it, if an incident causes a substantial disruption to the learning environment, if it is a repeated offense, or if it is statutorily mandated by law. Under those circumstances, I still have discretion, but the parameters change some.

When students are involved in significant disciplinary incidents, the principal refers to the incident as a bump in the road but not the end of the journey. Thanks to her, I find myself using the same analogy because it's true. It's never the end of the road; it's just a bump, and once you get past the bump, you can leave it behind since it's in the rearview mirror. That's how it works.

When problems like these arise, whether it's suspension, citation, or a nonofficial law enforcement action, I attend the school-based meetings with the student and their support team, which usually includes their caregiver, the principal, and the guidance counselor. I sit and listen, and then I share some words of wisdom. Since most of these incidents are cause for concern, we have to find a way to help that student avoid repeating them, which involves a deep analysis. In the meetings, we work as a team to try to help students identify better ways of managing these situations if they occur again in the future. Inevitably, students will continue to experience annoyances, frustration, or people they don't like throughout their lives. One of the goals of schools is to learn how to address adversity and social conflict with a healthy resolution. I love being part of the team that helps to map out healthier coping mechanisms than what brought the student to this meeting in the first place.

Let's say that a figurative "bump in the road" is a pothole. If you hit a pothole, you may get a flat tire. You don't throw the whole car away because of a flat tire. You fix it and continue driving. The same is true for students. Sometimes students do very dumb things, but you don't give up on them. You can explain what they've done is wrong and why they shouldn't do it, then you help them move past the mistake. It's better to move forward than fixate on the past. Our principal tells students not to get stuck in this rut by focusing on these moments. This statement resonates with me. When I visualize it, I empathize with students because we all make bad decisions at points in our lives, but we can't hyperfocus on a single event. It's okay to feel sad about a bad decision we made or even for getting in trouble for a mistake, but it's not okay to dwell on that sadness.

As a cheerleader for student success, you learn a lot about kids and their motivations. You end up learning who's trying out for the football team for the first time or who's trying out for the lead role in the school play. In the process, you become invested. You'll want to know when the next tryouts are scheduled or when the next game will be held. Students will fill you in and keep you updated when you show you're interested. They'll tell you how they lost the game because the other team cheated, and you sympathize with them, or they'll tell you they landed the lead role, and you'll cheer them on.

Most importantly, you'll learn to love what they love because it's important to them. These aren't skills we're taught in the police academy, but it's part of being a human and a good mentor for students. I tell my students all the time that I want them to be successful and productive members of society, but in order for them to achieve that, they have to feel good about themselves. That's why I cheer them on. As long as it matters to them, it matters to me.

Chapter 10: Leading by Example

As the saying goes, practice what you preach. For me, what I practice and preach is being honest with kids. It's a huge commitment because honesty is paramount in fostering relationships with my students. Years ago, we had a pretty heated situation in our community where there was a 911 call that resulted in someone barricading themselves inside a home. The SWAT team responded, hostage negotiators were involved, and the subject made his demands. During our debrief, the Chief made it clear to us that lying to the subject, under any circumstances, during the incident or anywhere outside of it, was unacceptable. Once you lie, trust is broken, and a lot can go south quickly if the other party discovers they were being lied to. This is why it's my life-guiding principle to never lie to anyone, especially not my students.

I found the best way to calm a situation is by removing the unknown. The unknown can be very scary, whether you have been involved in a car accident, victimized by a criminal act, or got in trouble at school. The fear of the unknown can make people act in unpredictable ways. There have been times when students have come to me after a long weekend of partying and told me they'd "been booked," which is just another way of saying they'd been arrested. They'll tell me they're scared because they think they'll go to juvie, also known as a juvenile detention center. They don't know what's going to happen to them, and it scares them. In most cases, I tell them they're thinking like that because they've been watching too much TV, which doesn't always depict law enforcement accurately.

When they tell me they "got booked" and explain what it was for (most often, it is for underage drinking), I explain what the upcoming process is going to involve, what they can expect, and what might happen if they are found guilty. I'm not minimizing the experience, nor am I normalizing or encouraging it. Instead, I'm encouraging them to own up to the mistake and accept the punishment they may receive. The punishment may come from the criminal justice system, their parents, the school, or all of the above. But as long as the student knows what to expect, they have the ability to think more clearly instead of worrying about the unknown.

In Pennsylvania, the issuance of a citation is a summary arrest, so it is more than just a piece of paper. When I have to issue citations, I always explain the process to students first to avoid any unnecessary drama during the arrest. I remind them I don't like issuing citations or arresting them, but it's a part of my job at times. I explain the process and what it means for them, as well as the different levels of crime and which ones they've committed.

An arrest for a more severe criminal act would look different because it might involve handcuffs, fingerprints, photographs, and then appearing in front of a judge. Though that's what most people assume, it doesn't always happen that way. That's why I take my time to explain the process. I explain the difference between the juvenile justice system and the adult criminal justice system, which takes a lot of tension out of the equation. Some parents come prepared for a fight, and most think getting a ticket or being arrested means the end of a better future for their child. They think it will prevent their child from getting into a good college or getting a job. I completely understand why they think that way, but once I explain how the juvenile justice system works and what happens when their child turns 18, they usually feel a sense of ease. In Pennsylvania, many juvenile arrests can be expunged from the child's record, giving them a "clean slate" in adulthood. Some parents have thanked me for taking these few minutes to explain the process to them and their children and what it means for their future.

As an extra measure, I describe how the courtroom setting looks. Unlike what is portrayed on television, the local courtroom is in an office complex. It has boring drywall, some plants by the window which have seen better days, and folding chairs in the waiting room. It's not the imposing marble structure we see on TV, and you don't always need an attorney, although you may want one.

Why do I do this? Because visualization helps people know what to expect and eradicates unpredictability. Have you ever imagined what a situation may be like, and then once you actually experienced it, realized it was nothing like what you had imagined? Wouldn't it have been nice if you had known what to expect going in? Understanding situations calms the nerves. I know it might take extra time, energy, and patience, but it's worth it. Intentionally not disclosing information to someone is also seen as lying, so giving these detailed explanations eliminates any possibility of them thinking I'm lying to them.

I'm not hiding in the bushes waiting to scoop you up or showing up at your house, breaking down the door, and dragging you out of your house. That's not what I do. Instead, I explain exactly what's going to happen, why, and how. In the event of any future law enforcement intervention, they'll trust me to inform them adequately because we've already established trust.

No one likes being arrested, and I try to avoid having to fight someone to arrest them. There is more power in using your words than there is in surprising someone and handcuffing them. Not only does it help to establish trust, but it helps to de-escalate situations and achieve the desired goal without causing additional unnecessary harm.

Another important component of this is treating students like real human beings. Oftentimes, people look down on children and want to establish their authority over them. I don't want that with my students. With all of my interactions, I treat my kids with respect, and respect is the only thing I ever ask in return. Sometimes, the students will horseplay in the halls. It's usually nothing aggressive or criminal, but they get loud and cause a disruption. They jump on each other, play fight, and yell. In a recent instance, I watched a group of students playing around and went over to talk with them. I knew each of them by name, and they all knew me, so my intervention wasn't a shock to any of them. All I said was, "Hey, guys. If you're somewhere you're not supposed to be, doing something you're not supposed to do, don't draw attention to yourselves. Don't leave trash around and don't horseplay. When you're loud, yelling, and dragging furniture around, you're asking for someone to catch you and get you in trouble." This is one of the many minor infractions I address and redirect throughout the day.

Well, my advice lasted for about thirty seconds before they got loud again and started jumping on each other's backs. That's when I put my Officer Beth voice on and told them they were being disrespectful. I said, "Knock it off. I am so good to you. I've asked you nicely to stop fooling around like this, and you're still doing it right in front of me."

They turned their backs on me and walked away, muttering loudly. I was so taken aback by the behavior that I called each of them by their names and told them they were being disrespectful, and I was not okay with it. I didn't yell or curse at them, and I didn't demean or chastise them, but I let them know the expectations I was holding them to. I said, "If you want me to treat you well, feed you, and overlook these minor infractions, I expect to be treated with respect in return. When I ask you to do something or stop doing something, you should just say, 'Yes, Officer Beth,' especially if it's nothing unreasonable." I told them I expected an apology from each of them.

Even though this interaction was upsetting at the moment, I also recognize these are teenagers, and it's a teenager's job to push boundaries and test limits. These are the times when I have to put on my Officer Beth voice and remind them how lucky they are to have an officer in their school, who treats them with respect and as real human beings.

Chapter 11: Smiling is Contagious

Elementary school students usually find the school environment new and a little confusing, especially because a lot is happening all around them. Every time I visit one of my elementary schools, the students are so excited when they see a police officer, but there are also times when some might feel a little strange or confused in the presence of law enforcement. Keep in mind, many of these kids are still adjusting to being away from their parents for the first time. They are exposed to new foods in the cafeteria, they are learning new skills in the classroom, and they are making new friends or learning who they don't want to be friends with. They may experience their first social conflict, their first loss at a game, being at the end of the line, or not getting the color popsicle they wanted. There are so many firsts happening in elementary school, and I get to help students navigate through them.

In the beginning of the year, SROs can plan for fun lessons in the classroom like talking about Halloween safety or the importance of wearing a helmet while riding a bike. Other than that, I like talking to my students about my role as an SRO. When I talk to them, using terms like "School Resource Officer" sound very official and formal, so I tell them I'm their police officer, and I love working with kids at school to make sure they're safe at all times.

When I do my first lesson with them, I start by asking very simple questions. I might ask them what I do for a living or who they think I am. I usually raise my hands above my head, spin around so they can see my front, sides, and back, then wait for them to guess. They shout out all sorts of answers: cop, policeman, policewoman, and police officer.

To challenge them, I'll say, "Nope, I am a fireman!"

In unison, they'll shout, "No, no, that's not true." or "You're the police!"

I smile because I know they're right, but I'll keep probing their tiny brains by asking questions like, "How did you know? What makes you say I am not a fireman?"

They'll point out everything they see on me that justifies their answers and yell out a gun, taser, walkie-talkie, badge, and keys.

Sometimes they'll ask questions unrelated to the topic at hand and ask if I know their older siblings or parents. Other times, they stray even further off-topic and tell long-winded stories. On more than one occasion, a student will raise their hand like they have a question. When I call on the student, I'll hear the narration in a squeaky kindergarten voice say, "There's this one time, my grandma and I went to McDonald's, and we were driving, and we saw this dog on the side of the road with a ball..."

Though it's adorable when they do that, I eventually stop them and redirect them with a simple instruction by reminding them a question should start with *who, what, where, why,* or *how* and end with a question mark. That's when they start asking questions about my police tools and how I use them. As I educate them about my role as a police officer, I explain how I keep them safe. In the process, I have to teach them about the different types of emergencies and how I deal with them.

I then ask them what they think my favorite tool is. They'll yell, "gun," "taser," "keys," or "walkie-talkie."

"No," I'll say, "My smile is my favorite tool."

Some students look confused, some are amused, and others cringe. Either way, it's always fun watching their expressions form. I tell them, "My smile is my secret weapon. Your smile is your best accessory, and the best part is, smiles are contagious! Not like COVID is contagious, but if I smile at Sam, Sam will smile back. Then when Sam looks at Jace, Jace will smile back. Then Jace smiles at Sasha, and, in no time, the whole class will be lit up with smiles."

The Missing Piece

Working with elementary students requires energy, patience, and creativity. There's no way you'll find me standing in one place while talking to them. I'm not presenting in a collegiate lecture hall; I'm in a class full of sweet, inquisitive, and highly energized students. I bounce from one place to the other, pointing at one student in the back left or standing by another student in the middle. Sometimes, I have to spice it up. We all know kids love their sweets, so all I have to do is spark a conversation about ice cream. One student will share with the class as to why she likes the vanilla flavor, and another tells a never-ending story about mint chocolate chip ice cream. The conversation spins from the least liked ice cream flavor to the most treasured. So, I pose this question to the class: "Does it mean we can't be friends anymore because Will doesn't like peach ice cream, and peach is my favorite?"

The kids usually shout out, "NO!"

Then, I ask, "You mean we can still be friends even if we don't like the same things?"

They all should, "YES!"

I teach them that even though we disagree on certain things, we can still be friends and get along with each other. I stress that it's okay to like what you like, to dislike what you dislike, and that it's okay if not everyone has the same preferences as you do. That's why there are so many different flavors of ice cream.

In most cases, elementary school students sense your energy and act accordingly. If you're gloomy and boring, they'll be gloomy and bored. If you're jazzed, hyped, happy, and engaging, you'll have the entire class involved. Clearly, I try to be the latter. Making the students smile, giggle, or laugh is my happiness. At the end of the session, most, if not all, of the students want to participate. It's my goal to make the lessons as interactive and educational as possible. Whatever we agree to discuss is exactly what we spend the time on, all while focusing on smiling and having fun. Not all of my lessons are about my role as a police officer. I integrate lessons about life in the most memorable and fun ways possible.

One time during a lesson, we were discussing emergencies. I started talking about my love for chicken nuggets, and I confessed to them the only way I eat chicken nuggets is by dipping them in lots and lots of ketchup. I actually do *love* ketchup, so I used that to my advantage by giving them a scenario with my favorite foods. I asked them if it would be an emergency if I ran out of ketchup in the middle of eating my chicken nuggets. A good number of them said yes. I was inclined to agree because I do love my ketchup!

Then, I asked if it was the kind of emergency where I should call 911. Thankfully, most changed their response to no. When I asked why, I got so many great answers. Instead, they suggested I dip my nuggets in honey mustard or get the walking tacos instead. They understood how to identify a true emergency, what to do, and what number to call. By the end of the lesson, after talking about ice cream, smiles, and dipping chicken nuggets in BBQ sauce, mustard, or even mayonnaise, some students started calling me Officer Ketchup. I embraced the name and impulsively bought a gigantic stuffed bottle of ketchup to carry around with me sometimes. The students seem to like Officer Ketchup, or at least, I think they do!

Most importantly, I create an opportunity for students to bond. My story acts as an icebreaker, paving the way for important friendships. Students who share similar likes begin talking to each other. These are the same kids who may have never interacted regularly beyond a hello. With this strong foundation, associating with each other becomes much easier.

My middle school students respond a bit differently to my duty belt. They like to ask questions about my gun or my taser, and they almost always ask if I can handcuff them. I tell them no because I love my job entirely too much. The instant someone sees me handcuffing a child at school without any reason, I would probably lose my job. Then they wouldn't have Officer Beth at their school anymore. Instead, I want to keep interacting with my students in the goofiest and silliest manner, to establish trust, and convey my intended message without violating any rules. If I can redirect the conversation away from my duty belt, I can engage them by focusing on something else.

I apply similar techniques with my high school students. For some students, seeing a police officer in uniform (even if it's me) might have the potential to make their hearts beat a little faster. Especially if they think they've done something wrong or have a guilty conscience. For students who don't like making mistakes or who rarely get in trouble, the look of guilt on their faces might be a dead giveaway. In those instances, I might just pause, say "Hey," make eye contact, and quietly ask, "Is everything ok? Wanna talk?"

There are times when I find students camped out, sitting in the hallways. Some sit by themselves, but more often I'll find pairs or groups. When I pass by, I smile, say "Hello," and ask, "What's going on?" They usually smile and let me know they're working on an English project or something like that. These interactions come in handy because they help me understand the culture of the school. An outsider might find it odd to see students lounging in the hallways during class, but that might be just a normal day for a particular school culture. Even though these interactions are light, casual, and conversational, they amount to a bigger picture. These little building blocks lay the foundation of trust in friendships and relationships within the school setup. They may seem insignificant on day one, but on day 180, they are quite important in understanding what is normal for our school. Recognizing what is normal allows us to recognize when something is out of the norm for the school.

Anytime you're in a school building, a friendly disposition can go a long way. Even when I'm on patrol and the situation isn't dire, I use my smile as my secret weapon. Many years ago, we had to arrest a drunk guy who was trying to start a fight with fellow bar patrons due to his intoxication and beer goggles. I tried to de-escalate the situation through conversation and with my smile since he wanted to fight my fellow police officers too. People tend to flow with the vibe I give off and the way I set the tone of interaction, so I used this to my tactical advantage.

This situation was resolved because I was able to talk with him while my coworkers handcuffed him. This way, the man didn't become confrontational, and no one got hurt. There's a big difference between walking into a room all smiley and happy versus hurrying into the same room with my hand on my gun and a stern expression on my face. Both instances depict different emotions and result in very different reactions. In the first scenario, people wouldn't think it to be a big deal because I look casual. In the second, everyone will be looking around trying to identify the person at fault.

So, smile more. What's the harm?

The Missing Piece

Mini-THON: Our school's dance to end childhood cancer

Policing the Bonfire Event

Dr. Beth J. Sanborn

Playing Mastermind with Elementary Students

Part III: Public Safety Educator

Up to now, it might seem like most of my days are a 10,000 steps per day walk in the park. I get to hang out in the safety of the school with my calming office space, and I get to have fun with the kids. For the most part, I would not argue otherwise. However, there is another component that comes with it, which I take very seriously. There are so many new trends in technology, social media, and drug culture that it can be easy for young people to throw their lives off course. Sometimes, the only factor standing between graduation and adjudication is one silly decision that could have been avoided with a little bit of knowledge and a trusted adult who they could bounce their ideas and decisions off of. My role as a public safety educator allows me the opportunity to support everyone in my district.

Chapter 12: Preventing Tragedy

An SRO's role as a public safety educator seems to get the least amount of attention in comparison to our law enforcement and informal counselor/mentor roles. I associate this with the fact that we are cops by trade, not teachers. We may find some discomfort in educating students because many of us don't like public speaking, addressing large groups of people, or being the center of attention. However, since teaching is inevitable, training is vital.

In police training, and more specifically SRO training, we learn the necessary skills integral to performing our job effectively. Adaptable communication is one of the many skills we use most often since we spend much of our days talking with our students and staff. As a public safety educator, I deal with all sorts of people, ranging from children to adults, who can all be in different emotional states. The lessons taught and language used with elementary school kids are not going to be the same as the ones used when addressing high schoolers or administrators.

When using communication skills, it is important to understand the different languages you can use based on your audience, and I am not talking about French, German, or Spanish. Though being able to speak other languages can help, it is not required to do this job. When dealing with high schoolers, I address issues like what to do when they get pulled over by the police, dealing with sexting, or the consequences of vaping. With middle schoolers, I might talk about cyberbullying or the health consequences of vaping. When it comes to elementary school students, we talk about lighter topics like being a good friend, bicycle safety, and community helpers.

Professionals in the education space know teaching children is not the same as teaching adults, but, too often, those in a law enforcement role don't make this connection. When it comes to talking to staff members, the approach is different because it's more direct. The content might be similar, but the context will vary. Sometimes I am required to educate them about the basics of the SRO's role because I want to ensure they understand that SROs are not disciplinarians or out to create a police state within the school. The staff shouldn't call me to classrooms to discipline unruly or disruptive kids. I am not a bouncer. I may be called upon from time to time for a disturbance between a student and teacher, but I don't maintain law and order just in that manner. There's a lot more I do within those four walls other than escort students out of their classrooms to the principal when they don't abide by the rules or monitor the noise level in the cafeteria.

For SROs, learning and educating comes in different forms and from different places. My first encounter with a student and a vape taught me a lot. I was photocopying some reports in the administrative suite one day when a teacher brought in a student who was suspected of vaping in a school bathroom. The assistant principal took the student's backpack, laid everything out on his desk, and started to search for the vape. He didn't find anything, but, as it turned out, he didn't know what to look for. So he requested I help the student pack up his belongings.

When the kid saw me, he tensed a little bit. Even though I wasn't a detective yet, his body language communicated something very specific to me – guilt. I looked at his personal belongings, and I didn't see any vape. However, I picked up a gadget that looked like a phone charger, and his facial expression told me it wasn't a phone charger. He was shocked, and his eyes were wide when I tried to hand it back to him. He was afraid to take it from me. To me, this confirmed his guilt. Eventually, we figured out that what I had in my hand was a vape. Obviously, at that point, we didn't give it back to him.

As a school resource officer, it is my responsibility to know what these things are. With the rapid technological advancements, it made sense why I wasn't able to identify it immediately as a vape. At that time, I was accustomed to vapes like the brand Juul, which resembles USB drives. This one looked more like a portable phone charger that was the size and shape of a stack of business cards. The fact that I couldn't identify it right away had me shocked and a little embarrassed as well.

I found this situation disturbing and viewed it as a failure on my part. I almost unwittingly handed a student back their contraband. As a School Resource Officer, I should be helping students make the right decisions and instill good morals in the process. I should be helping students make healthy and informed choices so they're able to be successful and productive people in society. If they're going to make a conscious decision to vape, they should be aware of its highly addictive properties. They should also know the dangerous effects the activity can have on their health and understand the legal consequences of using these substances. In Pennsylvania, if you're caught vaping under the age of 21, you could be cited and have to pay a fine between $100-$250 for a first offense, in addition to completing up to 75 hours of community service and a tobacco use prevention/cessation program approved by the Department of Health.

When it comes to educating parents, I opt to help them know what to look for in a child who may be experimenting with drugs and alcohol or who may be experiencing a mental health crisis. The goal is to be able to identify a child who may be approaching a crisis so that we can intervene before that crisis is reached. All of these measures are prudent in preventing tragedies from occurring. I don't ever want a student to feel like they don't have anyone to talk with if they're experiencing a crisis. Feeling alone may drive them into experimenting with drugs, alcohol, or other self-harming methods frequently used as coping mechanisms. Under no circumstances should any child feel like they're alone. When they get to such a mental place, they tend to think of the easiest way out, which may be alcohol or substance use, self-harm, running away, or even committing suicide. Because of the risks, it's vital to know what to look for in order to stop these tragedies from happening. If we identify one child who may be in crisis, maybe we can prevent it.

Chapter 13: Hidden

The vape my student had that day was hidden in plain sight. It was made in a form I had never encountered before. Even though it was right in front of our eyes, it was really hard for any of us to identify it. Vapes are probably the most innovative and concealable devices that have evolved over the years. If you think about a vape pen, it might look like a normal pen until you look close enough to realize you can unscrew the top lid to add the juice. Other variations of vapes look like candy containers or other colorful handheld items. Manufacturers intentionally make them this way, so students feel like they won't get caught.

I decided it was my responsibility to be more vigilant. When I was running errands on my days off from work, I found myself at convenience stores looking for products that were targeting children. What were these products? Where were they marketed? Some of the discoveries I made were shocking. I found a can of Arizona Iced Tea for sale for $15.00. I asked to see it, and when I looked closer, I realized you could unscrew the cap, stash something inside, and screw it back on. What a genius stash device! For an adult, expensive jewelry could be easily stashed in there. If a student wanted to hide cash, drugs, or a flask, this stash can is a good place to start. If you come across one, you'd think it was just a typical can of Arizona Tea. Once I started to critically analyze them and look at the places they were sold, I noticed smoke shops were the most common culprits.

When you don't know what you're looking for, the search is going to be hard.

I made it a point to start looking for hidden clues, hidden devices, and stash boxes. I found many of them were adorned with a marijuana leaf, the number 420, or a picture of musician Bob Marley. Instead of saying outright what these were, they adopted symbols referencing drug culture. Some of these devices came in the tiniest forms. I found a moonstone ring once, where you could flip the top open and stash a single pill in there where no one would notice.

When I spoke with parents, teachers, and social service providers, they all agreed they were uninformed about all of these new products. These devices are so cleverly manufactured that you can't blame them for not knowing. You may think your child is into cool jewelry, but they could actually be using it as a stash device and popping pills. That's why you need to know exactly what you're looking for, which can be hard when new items are coming out seemingly every day.

When I talk with adults about students who may be at risk, we can all agree that sudden changes in behavior should be looked into carefully. When a child's grades drop or they begin hanging out with a new clique that looks suspicious, it's better to be concerned and ask questions than do nothing and risk being sorry later. You might notice a sudden change in their interests or how they're expressing themself through their language, clothing style, or attitude. If your gut tells you something is wrong, go with it. Your intuition is stronger than you know.

The bottom line is, any change in your child's behavior, especially in a negative or aggressive way, should spark some questions. It may not mean a crisis is imminent, and it could be a harmless phase, but when it happens, seek more information. One change may mean nothing, but multiple changes may be cause for concern. Talk to their teachers, school resource officers, neighbors, and friends, but most importantly, talk to your child. Try to piece together relevant information in relation to your child's behavior.

Alcohol and substance abuse is not the only reason why a child's behavior could change, but it's good to be on the lookout for potential poor lifestyle choices. The only way to discern if your child is on the wrong path is through observing their behavior and having conversations about it. Never putting their backpacks down in your presence or not wanting you to touch something specific in their room could suggest they are trying to hide something.

Though drugs are the most common type of addiction in children and adolescents, it doesn't mean other addictions should be ignored. Some other addictions include caffeine, pornography, electronics, eating disorders, or self-harm such as cutting or burning. Most people wouldn't think twice about a child who carries erasers around, but they could be used to inflict self-harm by continuously and vigorously rubbing the eraser on their arms, creating heat through fiction. Here is a list of conspicuous ways children may be engaging in self-harm:

- Burning themselves with erasers
- Heating metal objects with a lighter to brand themselves
- Constantly scratching themselves or picking at scabs
- Punching themselves
- Pressing deeply on their eyes
- Snapping rubber bands on their skin
- Cutting themselves with razors.

If you notice your child is in possession of lighters, razors, pencil sharpeners, sharp metal, or rubber bands, ask them about it. It's important to be vigilant, and it's better to ask than ignore the signs.

Chapter 14: High

Back in the day, students were smoking in the bathroom. Heck, there's even a song about smoking in the boys' room. Because it was so common, adults would walk past the bathrooms and be mindful of cigarette smoke.

Nowadays, I hardly ever see a cigarette on our school campuses. Kids don't smoke cigarettes anymore. When I started to think about why they aren't smoking cigarettes, I thought about the millions of dollars of anti-tobacco campaigns and education that went into teaching them cigarettes were bad. Kids know they're dirty, they smell, and they cause cancer, so most students wouldn't even consider picking up a cigarette. Especially given how expensive they have become since most states have increased taxes to the point of making it unaffordable for someone with no income.

Vapes, on the other hand, use a different language. They have words like "juice" and "vapor," and they're flavored like orange, cotton candy, vanilla, or razzlemelon. Because these words don't sound as dirty or as dangerous as menthol or nicotine, they are more appealing to kids. There are a dozen different manufacturers who make a variety of disposable flavored electronic cigarettes in the most ridiculous flavors, many of which honestly sound delicious.

The look of vapes keeps changing from the Juul to a device that looks like a charger to a pen to a box of matches. In the initial evolution of vapes, I was finding flavored glycerin liquids, which were the original vape juices. I checked the label on each of the bottles to see whether or not it contained nicotine. At that point, CBD and liquid THC weren't even mainstream yet, but these juices were becoming more common and were found more often in schools. When I looked at the labels for the percentage of nicotine, I discovered it was much higher in vape juices than in cigarettes. So, even though we had a whole generation of children who never even considered picking up a cigarette, they were still becoming addicted to nicotine because of exciting juice flavors like Pineapple Crush or Fruit Loop Express. All of a sudden, this generation has unwittingly become addicted to nicotine.

We may joke about our addictions to coffee, soda, or chocolate because they've been somewhat normalized. We don't view them as harmful or think about the negative health associations, even though they absolutely do affect us physically. This is the same way kids viewed e-cigarettes when they first came out. They didn't realize the addictive properties, long-term ramifications, or how they were going to impact their health. They never realized they wouldn't be able to wake up one day and simply decide "I'm done vaping." It's already too late. Students are starting to feel those effects now in the form of withdrawal and cravings for another hit. I was really shocked to see this evolution from flavored glycerin to glycerin with nicotine, to high-nicotine concentrations, and now CBD and synthetic THC.

What is CBD? Well, all plants have chemicals in them. CBD is one of the chemicals in marijuana, but it doesn't have the psychotropic properties present in THC. THC is the chemical that gets you high, but CBD doesn't. Researchers, who have studied CBD over the years, have told us there are medical benefits of CBD. It is not yet regulated by the FDA, which is why you can find it in any and every product. It can be found in everyday items like soaps, lozenges, topical creams, tinctures, and even dog treats.

Eventually, these vape juices with fun, crazy flavors began to contain CBD in them. Even though it might not get students high, is it safe for them? There's no information on the proper or recommended dosage of CBD for a teenager. There could be different dosages depending on your sex, your weight, and your medical history. While I'm sure the dosage affects everyone differently, I just don't know to what extent. We don't even know what long-term effects there are yet.

The Missing Piece

The concern doesn't end at CBD. The same vape juices that contain CBD, nicotine, and/or flavored glycerin can also have THC in them. All of these items mimic each other in packaging, and students might not even know what they're ingesting. Adults certainly wouldn't know either, unless they read the labels. When we don't know what we are putting in our bodies, we risk getting high or having adverse reactions. To make matters worse, many students use these substances to self-medicate, but they're not doctors, and they don't know what they're ingesting or how much they should be taking.

The THC concentration in these modified synthetic products is significantly different from the THC concentration in the actual buds of a marijuana plant. It's definitely not the same as what people bought in the 1970s and kept in a Ziploc bag in their sock drawer. The two can't even be equated to one another. When marijuana advocates say you can't get addicted to marijuana because it's a natural plant that grows from the ground, I understand where they're coming from. However, variations like butane hash oil (BHO) or chemically-enhanced THC products are not the same animal.

There have been students in schools who are suffering instant seizures, panic attacks, hallucinations, lung issues, or other medical problems simply from taking one hit. It can be scary because we don't know what other chemicals are in these cartridges. It's like taking a sip from a random glass sitting on a bar – you don't know what's in it, if someone has tampered with it, or if it's going to interact with anything already in your system.

Because the look of marijuana has changed so much, we rarely find buds or even joints anymore. Of course, they're still out there, but we're finding more edibles now too. These edibles come in packages with bright colors and cartoon characters, mimicking childhood comfort foods, but they're laced with THC. How do you tell a kid how dangerous something is when it looks like it was made just for them? Without further inspection, the packaging helps these edibles slip right under the radar. Finding THC cartridges is equally as tricky. I only find these if students are walking around holding them or if they are caught by staff using them in a bathroom. They're so small and discreet, like the size of a pen or pencil, so it's very unlikely that I could easily find that on a student.

Although every school and region has its own issues with drugs, fortunately, my school district is not experiencing drugs like heroin, cocaine, or mushrooms. If we are, students are keeping it well below the radar. I often ask my students about the drug culture at the school, and they'll tell me about marijuana and pills. I had an interesting experience when I came to work on a Monday and found a medical emergency report involving one of my students from the weekend. The report read that he had a negative reaction to LSD, commonly called acid. I was shocked because I had never encountered a drug like that in my school before. I wouldn't even know what symptoms a student would experience from LSD or what to look for if concerns about that drug were raised.

I called my student's mom because I knew her well. I asked how he was doing and what was going on. I assured her that her son wasn't in any trouble and expressed my concern. I had her talk me through her weekend, then I asked if I could call her son to my office and talk to him. Again, he wasn't in any trouble, but I wanted to learn more about the situation. Mom gave me the okay, so I called him down and asked what happened. I assured him he wasn't in any trouble, but I wanted to know if LSD was a problem in my school because it was my responsibility to keep everyone safe. I used it as a learning experience for myself to find out where it came from. I have 1,400 students in the high school I am responsible for, so I needed to know if this drug was floating around and becoming part of the culture. It turned out he bought it in Philadelphia, and it wasn't something other students were using.

My next question was, what did it look like? I wanted to know what to look for if a student was suspected of carrying LSD. He described it as a little stamp the size of a fingertip. Then we talked more in-depth about the symptoms and other useful information like how he ingested it, what the effects were, how long they lasted, what the negative side effects were, how much it cost, and where it was kept. These were all important questions, and who better to get the information from than someone who has used the drug before? Honestly, if a parent were to have asked me what LSD looked like before that conversation, I wouldn't have known other than the understanding it looked like a generic stamp. I know what heroin, PCP, and crystal meth look like because these are drugs I have found when responding to police calls over the years, but not LSD. They may have trained us on it in the police academy, but that was 25 years ago, and drugs evolve.

In talking to that student, I was mostly concerned about his well-being and the fact that he was willing to experiment with drugs. Outside of that, I was concerned about all the other students in my building because it had the potential to be introduced to our kids and become a huge problem, especially since it was so small and easily hidden. This information was invaluable, and I wouldn't have been able to get it if I didn't have a relationship with that student and his mom. If neither one of them trusted me, if I wasn't a part of the community, or if I had lied to them at some point throughout my career, I would have never had access to this information. Building relationships is the best way to stay informed and keep my community safe.

Outside of these drugs, we do occasionally find pills like Xanax and Adderall, most likely because there's such a high prescription rate of them so they're easy to get. I don't know what the effects of these pills are, and I can't say for certain if some students are buying them because of self-diagnosed anxiety or if they're taking the pills recreationally. These pills are so small and easy to hide, plus they look like mints or candies. The size and similarities between pills and mints can often put school staff on edge. If a teacher sees a pill on the floor, they'll put on gloves and place it in a Ziploc bag – CSI evidence style – before they hand it to me.

Honestly, I can't identify pills just by looking at them, so I usually end up doing a Google search to see what it is. Sometimes, they are mints, and other times, they're antidepressants or anxiety medications. Although I can't hold anyone accountable when we find these pills on the floor, it at least gives me insight as to what is floating around the school.

When students sell Xanax on social media, they call them "bars," and you can buy a whole bar or a half for just a few dollars. Then, students make arrangements to meet up in the bathrooms or parking lots for the transaction. I was scrolling through Instagram years ago and saw a post from a few girls who were selling full bars and half bars of Xanax. They had discounts available for multiple purchases and a loyalty program for repeat customers. Though they had quite the business going, I turned it over to school administration and worked with them to communicate our concerns with the girls and their parents to ultimately put an end to it.

When parents think their child might be using drugs, they will ask me what to look for. I tell them they're probably not going to find the actual drugs or paraphernalia first. In fact, that may be one of the last pieces found. If they have concerns, I typically ask what behavioral cues or deviations from the norm they are seeing. It could be a change in language, who they're hanging out with, or very specific behaviors. If a child is usually accommodating and comes down for dinner at 5:58 because dinner is served at 6 then suddenly you have to call them downstairs multiple times, that's a little behavioral cue. They might quit activities they once loved. They might change friend groups, have a failed relationship or a new relationship, change their style of clothing or music, or even change the hours they sleep.

Those changes, in and of themselves, are innocuous and harmless, but when you start to notice multiple changes and patterns of behaviors, that might be cause for concern. Let's say your child has a new friend, which can be great. If the rule of your house is that you come in and take your shoes off, but this new friend doesn't want to, it might not be a big deal. Maybe that friend is self-conscious about their foot odor, and they don't want to take their shoes off. That's not a huge red flag. But if there is also a rule that backpacks should be left upstairs before going to the basement, and the friend refuses to take their backpack off, that might raise some alarms. If they're very protective of their backpack, that might not be a red flag, in and of itself, but it could also mean there is something in the bag they don't want you to find.

When you add everything up and put it all together, you may see a larger, more worrisome pattern. If their friend group changes, their grades start dropping, and they are overprotective of their backpack, that's usually an indicator that something is up. There are so many pieces to it. It's a matter of being observant so you can identify what's normal for your child and then what changes.

If you do suspect your child is getting high, talk to them. Try to have an open and candid conversation with them. But listen, that's in a perfect world where teenagers respond the way we want them to. If you ask your child flat out if they're getting high, their answer is probably going to be no. If you change the line of questioning to be more about their well-being, you may be surprised by their responses. Ask them if they've been feeling stressed or worried about school. Maybe they're feeling depressed about recent events in the world or something that happened at school. Sometimes we don't give children credit for having their own stances, but they feel the same stress adults do and aren't always equipped to deal with it the best way possible. So, if there are marital or financial problems at home, your child might feel that stress and look for a way to self-soothe because they are having trouble expressing themselves. When they choose to self-medicate, they don't realize it's not solving the original problem, and they certainly don't think about all the other complications it introduces.

As a parent myself, I know how difficult it can be to talk to kids, especially teenagers, but we can't be afraid to ask questions. I'm not suggesting asking your child if they're self-medicating with drugs, but you can say, "Hey, I noticed you're sleeping more than usual, what's up?" Sometimes asking an open-ended question like, "If you could change one thing right now, what would it be?" might be a way to get the conversation started.

If you're having trouble getting through to your child, try talking with the people who you trust and who know your child. Maybe it's a pediatrician, the next-door neighbor, your sister, their guidance counselor, a teacher, or a coach. It's okay to have a conversation with them and just let them know you're worried. If you don't know who to ask, talk with your child when they are in a good mood or happen to be chatty. Ask them, "When something good or funny happens, who is the first person you tell?"

There are resources in your schools and communities, and you can even look online just by searching "drug and alcohol resources near me." Your best bet is reaching out to your school guidance counselors because even though you, as a parent, might not know what options are available, the school undoubtedly will. Schools typically make referrals to resource centers and often use them for family support and assistance. What other people are more invested in a child's future than those who work in schools? They want to teach and help students grow to be healthy, successful, and productive adults. They are also familiar with different students who have struggled with different issues at various points in their lives, so they likely have more than one solution to a problem. They have a toolbox full of intervention plans, phone numbers, organizations, and people you can talk to for advice.

If all else fails, contact your local police department. Although the police departments can't promote one private organization over another, we can give you some guidance on what's available to you. Because police are social service providers, we often refer people to organizations for alcohol and drug prevention and recovery, mental health support, domestic violence support, internet safety, and elder services. Some people find it easier to call 911 rather than go to the local police station. Others may avoid contacting the police because they feel like they're bothering us.

I cannot state this more clearly – YOU ARE NOT BOTHERING US.

We're here and available, we're already working, and we want to help. If you have a question, problem, or concern, call 911 or your local police station. You can find the phone number for your local police with a quick Google search and by entering your zip code. If you call and ask us questions about drug and alcohol recovery for teenagers, we are NOT just going to come to your house and arrest you or call child protective services. That's not our job. We do more than arrest people. We're happy to answer questions for you. We have resources and can give you phone numbers, email addresses, and websites to look at.

Chapter 15: Hammered

There are a lot of programs out there warning teens about the dangers of tobacco use, drugs, and drunk driving. What I found interesting was that many teen interactions with police officers were happening over the weekends when they were experimenting with alcohol at a party or binge drinking. Alcohol is the most easily accessible intoxicant because it's legal for adults, and most parents have it in their homes. They can easily grab a beer from the fridge or pour some liquor into a bottle from their parent's liquor cabinet, and most parents likely wouldn't even notice.

It's not surprising at all that alcohol is the main issue among teens, so I knew it needed to be a focus of the program I was developing. The potential to abuse alcohol and become addicted is not a foreign concept because alcohol use is glorified as a staple of our society. For kids, it's taboo. They're intrigued by it, and they don't always make the smartest decisions with it. They might binge drink or experiment with a bunch of different types of alcohol. As they push those boundaries, they might be more inclined to experiment with riskier decisions like making "lean," which is a combination of alcohol, cough syrups, soda, and hard candy like Jolly Ranchers to make it taste better. If they can get it to match the color of a Gatorade flavor, there's nothing stopping them from bringing it into school. Some students just put straight, clear liquor into a water bottle, bring it to school, and hope nobody notices. When children start to engage in risky behaviors, they will keep trying to push the boundaries of that risky behavior because that's part of what they do when learning something new.

Just like with vapes and drugs, I needed to educate myself on what was out there in terms of alcohol because I knew there was more than just a six-pack of Budweiser that children could have access to. Now, there are tons of canned alcoholic drinks with cool labels. A can of Four Loko looks similar to a regular can of iced tea or an energy drink. Unless you really read the labels, you could very easily mistake a Four Loko or craft beer for some type of regular seltzer or other nonalcoholic beverage. As an SRO and a parent, it's startling because it's all easily accessible and easy to hide, which means it's easy to sneak into the house, school, or the Friday night football games. Not only that, but many of these edibles and beverages have a much higher alcohol content than your typical wine or beer. A normal beer might be 4.5% alcohol by volume, whereas a Four Loko is 14% alcohol by volume, which is over three times the amount.

As I continued looking, I noticed hard liquors and malt liquors had all these cool flavors as the vapes did. Adults who have ever been in the liquor store can probably easily name over 20 different flavors of vodka, and maybe at some point, you've been curious to try them. Some might sound gross, others might not be too bad, and some are better when you use them to make a cocktail. But, like vapes, when you have all these crazy flavors, they're usually meant to attract younger consumers. These flavors minimize a major hurdle to experimenting, which is the taste. When alcohol no longer tastes like paint thinner, it becomes more enticing. Just like medicine might go down easier when it tastes like bubblegum, alcohol goes down easier when it tastes like a coconut smoothie or a peppermint mocha. This blurs the lines on what kids think is appropriate for them.

On top of all the cool flavors, there are also alcohol-infused foods like gummies, candies, fruits, hot sauces, popcorn, and almost anything else you can think of. All of these edibles are meant to give you a buzz or get you intoxicated.

Kids are getting access to alcohol in a couple of different ways. They could be taking it from their home or their friends' homes. They likely know which spots in town tend to check IDs and which usually don't. They know which places to stand out front and offer somebody $20 to buy alcohol for them.

The Missing Piece

In Pennsylvania, beer is primarily sold in designated beer distributors, while hard alcohol and wine are sold in State-owned liquor stores. Even at the time of writing this, establishments that permit alcohol sales are increasing as laws evolve to permit these sales. If a store can prove they serve food and have a dining space, even if that means hot plates and folding tables, or grocery stores with dining tables, they may be able to sell packaged alcohol. In other states like New York, you can buy beer or malt beverages at any gas station, pharmacy, or bodega. Every state is different though, so make sure to stay on top of your local laws.

It doesn't really matter what the laws are or where the drinks are coming from though. If a child wants to get their hands on something, they will figure out a way. Once they have alcohol, transporting it is pretty easy. To the best of my knowledge, not many schools prohibit bringing beverages inside. You can bring a bottle of Gatorade or water anywhere with you. In fact, during the COVID-19 pandemic, we were encouraging students to bring their own bottles in so they could refill them from water stations, instead of using communal fountains. There's no monitor at the door checking water bottles for alcohol. Breath tests aren't conducted as students walk into the building or leave in the afternoon. School isn't a police state. There's an expectation that when students enter the building, they're there to learn academics, self-improvement, and how to make smart decisions, so while drug and alcohol education is part of the school curriculum, there's no focus on making sure alcohol doesn't come through the doors every morning.

That being said, we don't typically just find students with alcohol on them out of the blue. Instead, we are finding that, as the day progresses, a student may start to slur their speech or stumble while they're walking. Those are indicators for a teacher or adult in the building to have a reason for suspicion, which can then lead to a backpack check and finding the water or Gatorade bottle with the alcohol. Worse yet, we may find empty liquor bottles on the ground by the student parking lot, which gives even more reason for concern. This is where law enforcement in school comes into play.

As an officer, I have to be aware of the language I'm using when I talk to kids about alcohol. A few years ago, I was called down to one of the bathrooms by the cafeteria for a student who was throwing up. There was nothing overly unique or unusual about it, but I asked the student, "Have you been drinking today?"

Mid-vomit, the student said, "Yea."

I remember thinking, *Great, now I know what I am dealing with here.* So, I asked, "What had you been drinking?"

They replied that they had a bottle of water, some iced tea with lunch, and orange juice this morning. Then it clicked. I knew I was talking about alcohol when I asked if the student had been drinking, but that's not at all what the student thought I meant by "drinking." Once I realized the confusion, I explained what I meant, and the student hadn't been drinking alcohol. It turned out the student had a stomach bug, but I learned my lesson about being very specific with the language I use with students after that.

Aside from pop culture making alcohol appear socially acceptable, a lot of parents think it is too. I've encountered many parents who have the mindset, "If you're going to drink, you're going to stay here, in our house." When we have parents who know there is drinking happening in their homes and permit it, it can actually blur the lines even further for kids. Some parents think it's safer because the kids aren't out driving, but there are so many other tragedies that can happen beyond drunk driving.

A few years ago, there was a hazing incident at Penn State University where a student was drinking excessive amounts of alcohol within the "safety" of his fraternity house, but he fell down the stairs. His fellow fraternity brothers picked him up and put him on the sofa, without getting him any medical attention. The next morning when they woke up and checked on him, he was dead. He didn't go anywhere or get behind the wheel of a car, but he suffered a severe head injury as a result of a fall while intoxicated and didn't get any medical attention. Simply staying within the confines of a house doesn't assure safety.

As a parent, if you let your child spend the night at a friend's house, whether you're aware of any potential alcohol consumption or not, you expect your child to return home safely the next day. Imagine if your child fell and broke their arm, affecting their sports scholarship or their ability to play music. You'd likely be upset and want to hold that parent accountable. Allowing children to drink alcohol creates more opportunities for these accidents to happen. Although a parent might not be allowing them to get behind the wheel after drinking, bodily injury, financial loss, damage of property, or even death as a result of children consuming alcohol are still very real threats. Even though you think you're doing the right thing, or the "less wrong" thing, it's still not okay. Just as I do when I'm educating children, I have to put it into a different perspective for adults too. I know, as parents, you think you're doing the right thing by mitigating the negativity and allowing your kids to drink at home, but you can't allow it. You're still liable for it, and it's illegal. So, I often have to repeat the important lesson takeaways.

As a parent of a now 19-year-old and a 16-year-old, I get it. It's a difficult balance. When we took a family trip to Germany, both of my kids tasted beer for the first time. There was such excitement and thrill around the whole experience. When they finally tried it, they made the same yuck face I make when I drink beer because I'm just not a fan of it. When an experience like that is so taboo, it makes kids want to try it more. Being honest about alcohol, positives and negatives, can help deter children from wanting to try it so young.

Though I'm *not* encouraging you to allow your kids to try alcohol, I am encouraging you to have frank conversations with them about it. When the time comes, teach them what alcohol does to the body and the brain. There's a very specific reason why there's a minimum age associated with alcohol, which has to do with the formation of the brain and the way alcohol impacts brain cells. When you have these conversations, you can encourage good decision-making.

If you're concerned or have suspicions about your child drinking, I suggest keeping an eye on your alcohol stashes. I'm not suggesting you get rid of it – that's unrealistic. If it's something you enjoy, then you should be entitled to have it. When you do drink alcohol, model good behavior around your kids, set the standards of what you feel is appropriate behavior, and hold your kids to those expectations. For example, if you have a fridge dedicated to beer, have a conversation about it and be a good role model. If you're drinking 15, 20, or 30 beers every night and have absolutely no idea how much beer is left in the fridge, but you just keep replacing it, it's going to be difficult to track or monitor if your child is getting into your beer fridge. If you tend to only keep a six-pack, you're more likely to notice if one or two are missing.

The same goes for your liquor. Listen, it's not a secret that everyone from the 70s until today knows the trick of pouring out a little bit of clear alcohol and replacing it with water. Kids have done that since the beginning of time, but they can only get away with it to a point before parents realize the liquor no longer tastes like liquor. Another consideration may be using a locked liquor cabinet. That being said, a locked cabinet will only be as effective as the lock, so don't leave the keys in the lock!

It's all about taking inventory of what you have and being responsible, which comes down to modeling good behavior. If you're getting impaired and passing out every night, you're setting the stage and establishing that as acceptable behavior. It's going to be that much more difficult to break the chain of behavior or addiction with your child if they are seeing it from you.

The Missing Piece

I had a student who came to me and told me about his alcohol addiction. He was in AA and was super excited to show me his chip. When he fell off the wagon about three months later and was involved in a DUI crash, I showed up to his court hearing in uniform, even though I had no professional connection to the crash and subsequent arrest. I spoke with his attorney and told him, "I know that kid, and I adore him. Could I speak with him alone for a few minutes?" When I walked in, I just gave him the mom look. I didn't need to say anything because he already knew he let down a lot of people, which is tough and a huge burden on a child. We want our children to be focused on the future, whether or not they're going to get a new pair of sneakers for Christmas, if they're going to make the Varsity team, or where they're going to college. Breaking an addiction to alcohol shouldn't be one of the hurdles to their success. It shouldn't be one of the burdens they have to worry about. I'd rather have them worry about getting a pimple right before prom over worrying about making an AA meeting.

Though it's not unheard of for middle school students to drink underage, it's mainly my high school students who are drinking alcohol. When there are underage drinking parties on a weekend, no one likes it – not the cops or the parents. All of a sudden, there are 50 impaired teenagers who aren't thinking properly. As police officers, we've all had kids say things like, "I know my rights. You can't talk to me." Sometimes we even hear, "Do you know who my dad is?" or "Weren't you ever a kid?" or "Don't you have anything better to do?" We get all sorts of remarks thrown at us, and we have to laugh and brush it off, but this is why a lot of cops don't like working with kids.

Often police officers' only experiences with teens are during underage drinking parties on Friday and Saturday nights when kids can be obnoxious while impaired. It's usually late at night so cops are already tired. Let's be honest, nobody wants to spend three or four hours of the night shift handling the paperwork associated with an underage drinking party and having to call 50 sets of parents, then releasing those 50 impaired teenagers to parents who may be angry at the cops, saying, "Weren't you ever a kid? Didn't you ever drink before you were 21?" Remember what I said about modeling behavior? Although not all parents are like that, these are the experiences that sometimes make those relationships difficult. Then, on Monday morning, the students come into the school and tell me they got arrested over the weekend.

Although I see more high school-aged students using alcohol, it worries me that many of these students have younger siblings. While the younger ones aren't always experimenting with it, they are being exposed to it. Finding out their older sibling was at a party where the cops were called so some kids ran away from the house has the potential to influence them in the future. Sometimes older siblings tell their younger siblings not to tell their parents, and the younger ones think it's so cool. Again, it sends a conflicting message and blurs the lines for what kids think is okay.

If your child is drinking alcohol, there are a ton of resources out there to help them, and it is important to know everyone is on the same team and working in the best interest of the child. Drug and alcohol counseling for children is so prevalent because the science behind child development shows how children are prone to be impulsive and take risks. They're developing and learning, they are going to make impulsive decisions and experiment. You should expect your children to be exposed to alcohol and drugs in one way or another and be aware they might be curious enough to experiment with them. It could happen to anyone. A teenager could just be hanging out with friends, and one of them says, "Here, try this." Though some children may not even want to experiment with substances, they might not have the social skills or ability to say no. They might want to try out of curiosity or fear of being ostracized by their friends.

Not all kids are going to experiment and not all kids who experiment become addicted. When talking about gateway drugs, it's not necessarily a concern that using one substance will immediately get you addicted. It's not like you try a sip of vodka and you're immediately hooked and become an alcoholic. It's the experimentation mindset that can become dangerous. When you're willing to drink or do drugs again and continue a pattern chasing a high, that's when it becomes dangerous. When you're using intoxicants to self-medicate or avoid feeling certain emotions, that's when addiction can become a problem. That's no longer just experimentation.

Children are being exposed to higher alcohol by volume concentration and higher concentrations of THC or nicotine. It isn't unusual for marijuana to be laced with fentanyl, PCP, or formaldehyde referred to as "wet." It's not just found in big club cities like Miami and Los Angeles, like you may assume. It's driving through our towns, and it doesn't take long for these substances to trickle down into the school and into the hands of children who are predisposed to addiction issues.

Chapter 16: Mental Health Concerns

When I first became an SRO, I had no idea how prevalent mental health issues were in students. During high school, I thought guidance counselors were supposed to guide you into your career path and help you choose your college. It wasn't until I began working in schools that I realized they were dealing with crises all day long, from eating disorders, suicidal ideation, cutting, sexual fetishes, abuse, and neglect. I had no idea all that was out there, in my immediate community.

I'm aware my schools are no different from any other schools across America. No matter what type of environment you take a sampling of, when you have 1,400 children and adolescents together in close contact for a prolonged period of time, problems are going to arise.

Some students are medicated, some aren't, and some are self-medicating. Everyone has access to Google, and the first thing they do when they feel a certain way is Google the symptoms they're experiencing. If Google doesn't tell them it's cancer, it's going to informally diagnose anxiety, depression, ADHD, or another type of mental health disorder. That's when they start looking for ways to feel better and may turn to unhealthy coping mechanisms.

Some students may be so sad they experience suicidal ideation and enjoy the feeling of cutting or burning. While it's common for students with suicidal ideation to cut across their wrists, they also cut their forearms, thighs, private areas, and any other place on their body they feel they can hide. Some students take apart the small pencil sharpeners and remove the tiny metal blade inside to cut themselves with. As a parent or teacher, you probably wouldn't think twice about a student with a small sharpener because it's a seemingly normal, everyday object. One pencil sharpener is no big deal, but if you find a whole stash of them or the broken plastic of one in the garbage can, it's a good idea to start asking questions.

Students don't walk around with a spotlight on them, telling you who is suffering from anxiety, depression, eating disorders, or substance abuse. It can be difficult for students to disclose those issues, especially when they don't fully understand what they are experiencing. The school nurse has the access to find out if a student has been prescribed medication for diabetes, depression, and anxiety but has no way to check if they are taking them as prescribed. Unless a student tells you they have a mental health disorder, you can't exactly diagnose them. Nor are we, as SROs, qualified to treat even if they disclose this information to us. To complicate the matter, some behaviors of risk-taking or substance abuse overlap with symptoms of undiagnosed or misdiagnosed mental health disorders. This often makes it more difficult to tell if a student is engaging in potentially dangerous behavior out of impulsivity or if there are some underlying mental health issues.

Without building trust with students, they're not going to talk to you, and without building relationships with parents, they might not talk to you either. This is why it's critical to learn about students and their families and build those relationships. No parent is going to call you on day one and give you the full background on their child. However, if I know a student or a parent, they might confide in me that they experience anxiety. Personally, I don't hide that I sometimes feel anxious or go through bouts of depression because it's something most people can relate to at some point in their lives. Expressing this shows vulnerability and builds trust in relationships.

My daughter is the type of person to overanalyze and assume the worst, so when it comes to anything medical-related, she gets incredibly anxious. When I take her to the doctor, I tell the doctor she gets anxious even though she doesn't have a diagnosed anxiety disorder, and I ask them to explain to her what is going to happen. Removing the unknown has proved to alleviate some of the anxiety she experiences. I use that same practice with my students because I know it works whether they have a diagnosed anxiety disorder or are just feeling anxious about a test or an argument with a friend.

When I first started as an SRO, I had little police training or even experiences with mental health disorders beyond the occasional 911 call, but helping children came naturally to me, and I was able to determine what they needed at that moment. When I learned that NASRO offered a training called "Adolescent Mental Health Training," I jumped at the opportunity to learn more to best support my students.

As an SRO, we have to build relationships and take inventory of the resources available to us whether we gain them through professional training or in our own personal development. If a student comes to me and tells me the urge to cut is really strong today, I recognize I am only a bandage for the current crisis, and I can't fix their long-term pain. However, I will do what I can at the moment to help them by saying, "Thank you for trusting me enough to come in and talk to me about this. Let's get you in a place where you feel okay, and then we can move forward from there." I encourage them to focus on the present, not the upcoming AP test or what's happening this weekend. We focus on the right here and right now, minute by minute. We start off by taking deep breaths and progress from there.

Diagnosed, undiagnosed, and misdiagnosed mental health disorders are everywhere. I can't diagnose or treat – I can only support a student at the moment. I can pull in all the resources I have to help, but I won't be able to solve the problem long-term.

My school is incredibly fortunate to have a crisis counselor and a school psychologist because I'm aware not every school has access to these resources. I am part of the Student Assistance Program (SAP) team, which helps to identify students who may be struggling outside of the academic realm. I help with crisis plans on a case-by-case basis, but I'm not necessarily involved in every plan, nor do I need to be. I may be involved when there's a concern about drinking on the weekends or smoking marijuana, but I don't need to be brought into every conversation every time a concern is reported. If it escalates to a level of needing intervention or monitoring for an extra layer of support, I am included where it is appropriate. In the instances where I have a good relationship with the student or know about their history, it can be an advantage to have a friendly face in the room.

In Pennsylvania, schools have a Student Assistance Program (SAP). Even though some may call it by another name, the purpose is usually the same – to support students. Our SAP is a multidisciplinary team that gets a variety of perspectives on a particular student to remove barriers to learning. Any teacher or staff member can make a SAP referral, and we have boxes throughout the building where they can make an anonymous report or email a guidance counselor. For example, a teacher could report a concern about a child who has been sleeping a lot in class, when they've previously been very engaged. The teacher may have asked the student if everything was okay, and the student said yes, but the teacher is still concerned. When a referral is made to the SAP team, we come together and brainstorm who knows that student, what we know about them, what has changed, how their grades are, who their social circle is, and what may be happening with their family.

I am able to chime in if I'm aware of any police calls or records of social services being sent to the house. I might also have non-police-related information like if that student told me they started working part-time at a restaurant after school. I may know they are working from 4 pm - 8 pm to make a couple of extra bucks, then getting home, eating dinner, and doing their homework, then goofing off on their phone for a couple of hours before bed. Next thing they know it's 3 A.M, and they have to be awake in three hours to go to school. That would explain why the student is so tired. It might not be a great lifestyle choice or a great schedule, but it's a reasonable explanation for their behavior and less of a concern than what could be going on.

However, if we find out the student's parents just got divorced, and they're living with their mother out of a vehicle, not sleeping well at night because they're worried about sleeping in a parking lot with younger siblings, that's a different story. That's where we can intervene by reaching out to the mother and getting the family the support they need from a community partner or county agency. Perhaps the student just got into a fight with their former best friend and still has to sit through class and participate on a sports team with their now "public enemy number 1." This student can't help but think about this conflict, and it's showing in their behaviors, so we need to come together to offer support to redirect thinking and encourage a positive outcome. It could be bullying, poor grades, a recent breakup, or any number of reasons that we might not be aware of without open and honest communication.

Although there could be academic concerns, the SAP team takes on concerns surrounding mental health as well. When a student is struggling with mental health, it has the potential to impact their academics, but we can't know the scope of the problem until we start investigating. The SAP team intentionally has people from different roles on the team, specifically trained, so each of them can provide unique insight. These people could be coaches, teachers, the guidance counselor, the school psychologist, or the school resource officer. Everybody shares their little piece of information about a student to be able to put together that puzzle, identify the concerns, and figure out what is really going on under the surface.

Chapter 17: Piecing It All Together

Every single one of us shares a different facet of our personality based on who we're around. Much like how we, as adults, act differently around our spouse compared to our boss or how we act differently with our best friend than we do with our children, our kids have various facets of their personalities as well.

When it comes to conversations in school with the SRO, a parent's gut reaction might be to get defensive and combat the concerns by saying, "Not my kid." This reaction could be based on what the child is choosing to show to their parents at that time. While nobody is going to know a child better than a parent or caregiver, there are always going to be those missing pieces. There are so many other aspects of their personality a child is going to show to other people like their friends, teammates, teachers, and even strangers. They may show off different sides of who they want to be to each person they encounter in a different role. Think about how you might hide a secret from one person, but you might be very willing and forthcoming to share it with someone else.

It's so critical that, as adults, we share those little pieces of information about a child with each other to get an overall picture of who they are and how they act in all situations. Sharing this information strengthens the safety net we're building because we are able to see a clearer picture of a child's overall personality and behavior. Only one person's perception and knowledge of a child might not be sufficient enough to truly identify what's going on under the surface. Once we start to combine all of that knowledge, we might find out about interests a child has which may be different from the interests they typically express to a specific group. One set of interests may not be applicable or acceptable to a different group, so a child is constantly expressing different facets of their personality.

It's impossible for one person to see and understand all of the different layers of a child, no matter how well we think we know them. They might be very superficial in one relationship, whereas they could be really, really deep in another. By combining all of the aspects of a child's personality together, we can really identify who a child is at their core and provide better support.

When I facilitate Hidden, High, & Hammered and talk about stash devices, drug paraphernalia, alcohol, and poor lifestyle choices, those might be things a parent or a caregiver never sees around their child. A child is not going to be open with contraband they know they shouldn't have – they're going to be hidden. What's not hidden are the changes in their interactions, their behaviors, the language they use, and the hours they are keeping. It might be difficult for a child to actually verbally communicate, "I'm really struggling, and I need help," but they are likely to communicate it through their behaviors. It might be through withdrawal from relationships, a change in friend groups, or a decline in grades. When parents ask me what to do, what to look for, or what the telltale sign is, I tell them there is no telltale sign of a child who might be in crisis until it is too late. If a child is picking up a razor blade and they're cutting themselves, there has already been a tipping point in that crisis, and they need immediate intervention. At that point, we've already missed the signs, and they might need long-term care, therapy, or hospitalization. When this happens, we need to reestablish and strengthen their support system.

The goal is to strengthen our network so we can intervene before the crisis is reached. That's why we need to look for those other behaviors signaling a crisis, instead of simply focusing on hidden stash devices or alcohol. As I've said, kids are going to do dumb stuff. A single, isolated incident might not be indicative of a crisis; it might just be a result of adolescence. They could simply be experimenting to figure out what kind of person they want to be, who they want their friend group to be, or what's going to be important to them. We have to make sure we don't ignore those behaviors or become hyper-focused on only one piece of the puzzle.

The best proactive approach you can take, first and foremost, is talking with your child. Set expectations, listen to them, and I mean really *listen* to them, and understand that, even as preteens and teenagers, they have opinions and preferences, and they're entitled to have them. It's actually pretty cool when you get to learn who your child really is through reciprocated respect. It's exciting to see a child develop into their own person, rather than just becoming a mini version of you. When you can have an adult conversation with your child in a safe space where they can share what's important to them, it's really neat. You start to understand they are going to be a real person, and you've helped to raise them to become a productive member of society. My best advice is always to talk to your children when you have concerns or notice a change in their behavior.

Though I'm not suggesting you go into your child's room every night and start snooping around, sometimes it's worth just taking a look around as you're doing laundry or straightening up. Nothing is more divulging about someone's personality than their bedroom because it's a personal, safe space.

My next piece of advice is to talk to other people who know your child. Share information about your children with each other so when you do have these concerns, you're not sitting at home wondering, "Is my kid in crisis? What do I do about it?" You should know your child's guidance counselor's name and their favorite or least favorite teacher. You should know if your child has someone at school who they can connect with or talk to. Does your child have a good relationship with their coach, their religious leader, an adult family member, or with the next-door neighbor? Share any concerns you have with them and encourage those healthy relationships.

Establish the boundaries of a healthy relationship with your child. Sometimes, there might be a little bit of give-and-take like pushing the curfew out a little later, giving a bit more freedom with screen time, or allowing them to make mistakes that aren't going to be irreparable in their lives. We can't hover like helicopter parents. We can't be Marlin from *Finding Nemo* and never let anything happen to our kids by sheltering them from the rest of the world. As Dory tells Marlin, "Well, you can't *never let anything happen* to him. Then nothing would ever happen to him." The same is true for our kids.

There has to be a balance though. As parents, we don't want to be so hands-off that they're left to fend for themselves. It's okay for a kid to fall, skin their knee, and get hurt. It's okay to have an accident and get burned. It's not okay for parents to be completely hands-off, not set boundaries, or fail to act as a buffer to help guide them. Sometimes we have to be the bumpers at the bowling alley, but it's okay to give them a little more space in the lane.

If you have concerns, if you feel like your conversations aren't going anywhere, or if you see troubling signs, it's time to reach out for help. What you might find is that someone else probably noticed a change or different behaviors as well. Imagine a snowball starting to roll downhill. When you pull in one person, then they can pull in another person, and then another person, and that network grows stronger and wider. You then have all these different people who know your child and can provide more context to what's going on with them.

This is another reason why the Student Assistance Program (SAP) is such a great resource. With SAP, we have access to all of these people who get to know your child. In some cases, the parent or guardian might have to be the facilitator, the quarterback, who pulls the team together. They may even have to bring in some outside people and get everyone to the same table, perhaps their therapist, coach, a neighbor, their employer (if the child has a job), or even their best friend and their best friend's parents.

The Missing Piece

If you start to have concerns, trust your gut. It's a really powerful sense, and if you think something is wrong, you're probably right. For parents who feel their child is "too far gone" or that they can't build a relationship with their child, it's never too late. I fully recognize that's easier said than done. There's a sign up in my office that says, "It's not a sign of weakness to admit you don't have the answer." As a parent, if you're struggling to connect with your own child, maybe you need to call in reinforcements, and that's nothing to be ashamed of.

As a mom, when I can't talk to my daughter, I might enlist the help of my husband because maybe he can better connect with her. Don't be afraid to pull in the child's aunt, uncle, grandparent, or anyone close to them. Because they have different relationships with different people, they may be more likely to open up to someone else.

Sometimes, taking a step back can afford you the time and the ability to look at situations a bit more objectively and less emotionally. You might not have that answer, and that's okay, because it truly does take a village to raise a child. If you are struggling to connect with your child, ask a family member or close friend to intervene. Depending on the relationship you've built with their friend's parents, you can always ask them to step in and just say, "I noticed you seem different. You seem sad or troubled. What's going on?" That might be enough of a reset or a way to at least create a safe space.

As a parent, you don't always have to have the answer, but you should have some options for where to go to find an answer. That's where you're going to have to rely on your team. That's where you need someone in your corner who has access to the resources, the names, and the information you need. That's where an SRO can help you.

It's an SRO's job to know where to find what you need and know who to connect you with. Rather than throwing our hands up and saying it's too late, we can try saying, "I might not have the answer, but let's find someone else who does." It's never too late, and our children are always worth trying for, again and again.

The Missing Piece

Unity Walk Organized by a Former Student

A Sampling of Hidden, High, & Hammered

Dr. Beth J. Sanborn

Keynoting from the Big Stage to More Than 1,000 SROs
and School Safety Partners

About the Author

Dr. Beth Sanborn is a police officer, speaker, youth advocate, and the founder of Hidden, High, & Hammered LLC. She joined the Lower Gwynedd Police force in 1997, and currently serves as a patrol officer. In 2015, she assumed responsibility for all juvenile cases, earning her the rank of Juvenile Detective while she served as School Resource Officer (SRO) until August 2022.

Beth earned her bachelor's degree in criminal justice and sociology from Widener University in 1996. She later earned her master's degree in criminal justice from St. Joseph's University in 2014 and her doctoral degree in public administration from West Chester University in 2019 where she completed her dissertation entitled "School Resource Officers as Mentor/Counselors, Including Levels of Intervention".

Beth sits on the executive board of the Pennsylvania Association of School Resource Officers (PASRO) and is an instructor for the National Association of School Resource Officers (NASRO). She most recently was appointed to various committees at the International Center for Law Enforcement Studies, and actively volunteers with the Montgomery County Office of Children and Youth and Mission Kids Child Advocacy Center.

As the founder of Hidden, High, & Hammered LLC, Beth's mission is to educate parents, teachers, and social services providers about the indicators of drug use and abuse as well as other poor lifestyle choices among teens. Her program stresses the importance of communication across the invested stakeholders in teens' lives, so we can identify a teen who may be in crisis and intervene before that crisis is reached.

Aside from her passion for supporting youth, Beth is also a mother to two amazing teenagers and is married to her husband Andy, who retired from the Upper Dublin Police Department after a successful 25-year career. She also has an incredibly annoying dog, who has claimed her as "his person."

To learn more about Beth's work and Hidden, High, & Hammered, visit www.bethjsanborn.com.

Made in the USA
Columbia, SC
24 April 2024

34847186R00085